Den + Jeanne —

With Best Wishes

You favorite

Bonner

Ray

6/1/09

Creating Your Legacy

A Do-it-Yourself Guide for Baby Boomers*

by

Raymond W. Empereur

*For and about the <u>Baby Boom Generation</u>, defined as the 77 million Americans born between 1946 and 1964

INFI∞ITY
PUBLISHING.COM

Copyright © 2009 by Raymond W. Empereur

ISBN 0-7414-5417-3

Published by:
INFIꙨITY
PUBLISHING.COM
1094 New DeHaven Street, Suite 100
West Conshohocken, PA 19428-2713
Info@buybooksontheweb.com
www.buybooksontheweb.com
Toll-free (877) BUY BOOK
Local Phone (610) 941-9999
Fax (610) 941-9959

Printed in the United States of America

Published May 2009

ACKNOWLEDGEMENTS

I would like to thank my family, many of whom are pictured above, for providing the inspiration for this book.

Special thanks also to my wife, Sherry, who spent many hours reviewing my work, and to my sister, Jean Hotopp, who also helped with editing the manuscript, providing comments and helpful suggestions.

Thanks are also due to Infinity Publishing for a fine job of converting my manuscript into the attractive book it has become.

Finally, thanks to you the reader for purchasing this book. It is my hope that you will find value and enlightenment in this little volume.

Introduction

So, you are a member of the great American Baby Boom generation, that is you were born between 1946 and 1964... and you are feeling like leaving something behind for your kids, grandkids, and great-grandkids. You want to leave something personal and unique, not just money and possessions. Great! Leaving behind something personal and lasting is not difficult.

Why not create a personal written legacy to gift to your heirs? It's easy and you probably already use a PC, right? Chances are you know your way around a keyboard too. Good. Let's get started.

This little book is a "two for one" bargain. I've created numerous brief personal family essays to share by example, suggesting a pathway for your own creativity. And this book contains something unique:

You'll find helpful notes and spaces for notes that you can make to begin creating your own set of personal reflections and essays – a memoir for you to convey to your loved ones, and a record for future generations, yet unborn, who will inherit your bloodline and something most of us never get to know about those who preceded us.... A glimpse at your thoughts and dreams, personally recorded just for them.

This book is meant to provide you with a template to create a written legacy through short personal essays about your life and times. I've shared my own personal essays as examples, and have left space for your own notes, as a prequel to preparing your own essays.

The work that follows suggests a number of themes, as identified in the essay titles, and you can use these, or more appropriately you can make up new themes to write about. The only limit is your own creativity. I've chosen to produce essays with positive, life affirming messages.

Heaven knows life provides too much serious or unpleasant stuff to deal with, and lots of negativity too. But, I've eschewed the negative and hope my contemporary family and my heirs, present and future, will think of me with admiration, humanity and humor. Why not, most of life can be pretty wonderful if you let it be.

So read on, and if you are of a mind to create your own written legacy, please don't put it off for too long. Use this little book as a beginning and a guide, making your formative notes in the white spaces and margins provided. And remember your writings can be preserved forever in various electronic formats, and on paper too for that matter. And you may choose to include photos as well. Be as creative as your talents and imagination allow.

Way back in 1996, I finished my own little book and gave it to my mother for her and my dad to enjoy. That was in May, Mother's Day, to be exact. I was just 49 years old back then.

I called the 1996 unpublished book: *Between Thirty – Something and Eternity: The Baby Boomers at Mid-Life.* I wrote it mostly for fun, but with a glimmer of hope that I might get it published, someday. However, I never really tried to publish the book. This time is different. This book, while based upon my original work, is *new and improved* as well.

Here's how I presented the manuscript to my Mom, on the first page, bound in a simple three ring binder:

To Mother

This little book is my Mother's Day gift for you for 1996.
I've been laboring over its contents intermittently now for
over two years.
Maybe it will be worthy of publication, but probably not.

What's important is that it's done... at least for the time
being.

More important is that this collection of words is a credit to
the careful nurturing and unconditional love that you
shared with me during my childhood.

The values you demonstrated by example will remain with
me forever!
Thus this little book is a positive life-affirming statement
filled with hope, optimism, and a little humor....

Thanks Mom!

It's Your turn: *OK, here is how the format works. The space that follows affords you, the reader, an opportunity to make notes about creating your own family story, in a format of your choosing, as short or as long as you want.*

How would you begin? How would you dedicate you work? Make some notes below, and then begin to form your own set of essays, or use a different format, one to your liking.

Any word processing software will make your task easier. Be sure to save all your work to some form of electronic storage. (I used a flash drive.)

Once begun, go back to the work as you feel motivated to do so. And take your time... I labored for two years before finishing mine in 1996, and now I'm revisiting the whole project.... To make it better and more complete, and to share it with you, as well as with my family.

Your notes:

_____

_____

_____

_____

_____

_____

_____

_____

_____

_____

_____

_____

_____

_____

_____

_____

_____

_____

_____

_____

_____

_____

_____

_____

_____

_____

Are you into family genealogy? Have you ever wanted to know the names of your ancestors?

I believe that someone in each family <u>should be</u> responsible to research their family story. It's fun and life affirming too.

Read on for more information on completing a family genealogy. This format provides an excellent place to tell the story of your family. Make more notes:

_____

_____

_____

_____

_____

_____

_____

_____

_____

_____

_____

_____

_____

_____

_____

_____

_____

_____

Now, by example, back to my story...

In the 1990s I wrote my book in *MSWorks*, and since then, moved on to *Word*, and have lost or misplaced the diskette which contained the original book. <u>Don't make this mistake</u>. In addition, the computer used to produce the book was the victim of an electric surge that fried the hard driver. So much for my book!

We moved in 2005, and disposed of many unneeded items. It's possible I discarded the only diskette. At any rate it's missing. Thus I only have the original paper copy that I gave to mother 12 years ago. (Don't make my mistake. Be sure to store and keep your book in some kind of permanent electronic storage!)

Mother passed away suddenly in 2000 and thank goodness we found the original book among her personal effects. Dad, also a member of the World War II "Greatest Generation", returned the book to me and lived on until late in 2007, passing on, as they say, at the ripe old age of 88 years and three months.

He was the youngest of five siblings, outliving all the others. He died from old age and from dementia and heart disease. But mostly, his body had just worn out. For most of his long life, dad was very healthy and vigorous, but he slowly declined after mother passed away. Dad had a long and full life, most of which he enjoyed. I hope for the same.

I've decided to reprise my 1996 book, which was never published, in this new format, and to update it with a fresh, and more mature, view of the Baby Boom generation, some 77 million strong born between 1946 and 1964. I'm among the first wave of Boomers, born just nine days into 1947, less than a year after dad returned from service in World War II, to be reunited with mother and my older sister in 1946.

_____

_____

_____

_____

_____

_____

_____

_____

_____

_____

_____

_____

_____

_____

_____

_____

_____

_____

_____

_____

_____

_____

_____

_____

_____

Returning to my work….

About this little book of personal reflections:

Are you a "Boomer"?

A Baby Boomer is someone born between 1946 and 1964 (more or less). Chances are, with over 77 million American Boomers on the scene, you are one of us… or are close to one by parentage, siblinghood, or marriage!

This book is about Boomers, from the perspective of one who **Is.** Herein, you will discover some of what makes us distinct… some of what makes us unique. We are like every other generation, and we are very different as well!

This may not be the definitive work on our group, our demographic, but the short essays will, I hope, stimulate reflection, and may cause you to smile. That's my hope.

For you see, we're a lot alike…We Boomers.

NOTES: And as you know, this book is also a primer, and a guide for how you may want to create your own story. Would you write a "Dedication" for your collection of personal family essays? Mine is discussed on the following pages, as an example.

_____
_____
_____
_____
_____
_____
_____
_____
_____
_____
_____
_____
_____
_____
_____
_____
_____
_____
_____
_____
_____

Dedicating Your Work

My 1996 Dedication named my grandfather, our kids and one grandson as well as my parents and someone named Larry Berlin, who mentored me into creating a personal journal back in 1990. At that time I was working on an advanced degree in public health at the University of Michigan, as discussed in Essay Twenty-Three. I've been keeping a personal journal since 1990, and this format has grown to several hundred pages and will also be available to my heirs.

More than 12 years have passed since 1996 and you might suspect that the march of time has added more grandchildren. Our son, Chad, and daughter, Marci, have both married and have provided us with more babies to love. So in addition to Sean, Chad's first son, allow me to add and introduce his younger sister, Michaela, and infant brother Lucas, as well as his cousins, Delaney and Jace, daughter Marci's two children.

Sherry and I are the proud grandparents to five: three boys and two girls, ranging in age from 11 months to 15 years. Therefore, I am pleased to dedicate this revised and improved book as I did in 1996, with the addition of <u>all five</u> of our grandchildren: Sean, Michaela, Delaney, Jace, and Lucas. The dedication follows on the next page.

Room for notes:

DEDICATION

To My Boomer Family and Friends;

To Martial J. Empereur, my paternal grandfather, who admonished me to become well educated;

To may parents Louise and Ray, who implanted durable values;

To my life's partner, Sherry, who shares many of my dreams; and

To Our Kids, Chad and his wife Dawn,
And to Marci and her husband Scott,
And to their children,
Our precious grandchildren –

Sean, Michaela, and Lucas Empereur,
And
Delaney and Jace Morris

The future belongs to you.

If you were to write your personal memoirs, how would you compose your dedication?

_____
_____
_____
_____
_____
_____
_____
_____
_____
_____
_____
_____
_____
_____
_____
_____
_____
_____
_____
_____
_____
_____
_____
_____
_____
_____
_____
_____
_____
_____
_____

Next, a few paragraphs about the author are in order…

About the Author

Born in January 1947, Ray W. Empereur is among the "first wave" of Baby Boomers.

Ray and the former Sharlene B. Hunt, married in 1966, and have raised two children, Chad and Marci. A career public health administrator, Ray took an early retirement from County government at the end of 1997, to pursue a doctorate and find his own way as a part-time college teacher and consultant.

He returned to full time work as an agency director in the private non-profit sector in 1999, and "retired" again in 2006. He is currently self-employed as a health and human services consultant. Real retirement is likely a ways off.

Ray and Sherry live in rural Winnebago County, Illinois, just west of Rockford, with Daisy Mae, one very special old female calico cat. Ray is the self appointed Empereur Family Genealogist (since no one else wanted the job), and produces a family newsletter four times a year.

Sherry and Ray share a hobby - they are Civil War Reenactors and living historians as well, having been active in the 8th Illinois Cavalry (the Federal side) and the 9th Virginia Cavalry (the Confederate side) with McGregor's Artillery Battery.

This is Ray's first book.

What would you write about yourself, as the author of your own set of personal reflections?

_____

_____

_____

_____

_____

_____

_____

_____

_____

_____

_____

_____

_____

_____

_____

_____

_____

_____

_____

_____

_____

_____

_____

_____

_____

_____

_____

_____

_____

_____

_____

_____

Next, you'll need a table of contents...Like this one:

Most Boomers have by now, departed from the radical thinking and alternative lifestyles characteristic of the 1960s. We have "bought" and settled into the American Dream, mostly in the metropolitan suburbs we helped create and populate. Once at one with Hippie culture, we have matured to pursue careers, own property, pay our taxes, complain about government, and are loyal red blooded Americans, participating in church and community, and usually voting when called upon.

We are stakeholders too. That is to say many millions of us are military veterans and are small-scale capitalists, owning commercial enterprises, stocks, bonds, and mutual funds. Many have amassed significant wealth, much of it transferred from our parents as they have passed on a monetary or property inheritance.

While few are "rich" in money assets, most are comfortable and middle-class. We are thus a cross-section of America at her best and worst, and a big section at that. In fact, like it or not, Boomers are now for the most part, in charge of America. Right now, people over 55 own 77% of all financial assets in the United States. And adults over 50 account for 45% of U.S. consumer spending, a whopping $2.1 trillion per year.

That's right, like it or not, the generation that disrupted the 1968 Democratic Convention, smoked pot and burned bras, participated in the "Counter-Culture", occupied the offices of college presidents in opposition to the War in Vietnam, and those who chose to serve honorably in that conflict, have taken over the United States. We are firmly in charge. Forty-one percent of American adults are now over 50, the highest percentage in U.S. history.

Just look at the people who populate Congress, where the average age is 60. In fact, 80% are over 50. Look at your Governors, your City Councils, the Military Brass, Corporate leaders. And yes those who recently sought and won the Presidency, starting with Bill Clinton, George W. Bush, and now Barack Obama are all Boomers. Fully half of all Americans who voted in 2006 were over 50.

The Greatest Generation has passed into retirement, and many by now have passed away, leaving us in charge. By 2011, Americans over 50 will surpass 100 million people. And, we have been reshaping America since we first began appearing in large numbers:

- The Baby Boom was launched in 1946 by an onslaught of "Victory Babies" parented by GIs returning from World War II;
- The babies kept on coming all the way through 1964, an era marked by the birth of the American Middle Class, and framed by the Cold War, and the looming threat of nuclear destruction;
- By 1950, suburban development was well underway to provide the new homes and shopping malls, parks and schools, needed to contain millions of new families and fuel their consumer demands, born of unprecedented prosperity;
- In 1951 the first Boomers entered school, resulting in a building boom in expanding public education facilities nationwide;
- Boomer families were the first generation to enjoy enough prosperity to make middle-class vacations possible, and Walt Disney built his California Disneyland which opened in 1955, as a dream vacation destination for millions of Boomer families. (I was there too, back in 1960, thanks to the growing interstate highway system);
- Baby Boomer births soured to 4.3 million in 1957, the peak year;

- By 1960, the first Boomers were entering puberty, and, aided by the introduction of effective chemical birth control, the Sexual Revolution was born shortly thereafter;
- 1964, the last year of the Baby Boom, witnessed 4 million births;
- The American Viet Nam War, 1964-1973, was led by elders but fought mostly by Boomer GIs, while other Boomers protested vigorously. By the end of US involvement, 58,000 were dead, and 158,000 wounded;
- In 1968, Martin Luther King, Jr. gave his famous "I Have a Dream" address from the steps of the Lincoln Monument in Washington DC. Thousands of Boomers, Black and White, were there and millions have since struggled to bring about racial harmony. Barack Obama won the nomination of the Democratic Party, seeking to become the next Boomer to occupy the White House, and the first man of African heritage to do so.
- Sarah Palin, a forty-something "hockey mom" and Alaska Governor, also a Boomer, aspired to be Vice-President, had the Republicans won in 2008.
- The Woodstock (New York) Music Festival drew 460,000 Boomer youth in the summer of 1969;
- In 1975, Boomer Bill Gates, born in 1955, quietly formed Microsoft;
- In 1981, the world was introduced to AIDS;
- The Vietnam War Memorial opened in Washington, DC, in 1982.
- Boomer Michael Jordon, born in 1963, joined the NBA in 1984;
- In 1991, Clarence Thomas, born in 1948, became a Supreme Court Justice;

- Bill Clinton, born in 1948, is the first person born after World War II to be elected President in 1992;
- By 1994, Boomers were making their presence known in the 104th Congress, constituting 44% of members.

The past sixty years have witnessed profound changes in American life and culture, much of it attributable to the influence of the Boomer generation. Read on. In the collection of brief essays that follow, you may glean a bit more knowledge about our generation. And, I hope a few shards of wisdom, too.

Ray Empereur – Spring 2009
Rockford, Illinois

Notes: *More space for your own reflections and notes. Ready to start your own set of personal essays? My first, "Time in a Bottle", follows.*

_____
_____
_____
_____
_____
_____
_____
_____
_____
_____
_____
_____
_____
_____
_____
_____
_____
_____

Essay One: Time in a Bottle

To every thing there is a season, and a time to every purpose under the heavens...
Ecclesiastes, 3.1

For a long time now, I've enjoyed writing for pleasure, beginning with keeping a personal journal, which I began back in 1990. If asked, "Why do you want to write about life at middle age?" I can summon four basic reasons. I'll recite, then briefly expound on each:

Reason No. 1 – Mastery of the Media
In the first place, like many aging Baby Boomers, my work, "my profession", has taught me how to write. That is, the work I have done much of my life involves using words on paper as a work product for which I'm paid – and rather well at that. I've transitioned from doing "body" work like that of my Dad, to doing "mind" work, like that of most people educated at the Bachelors level or beyond. Thus many Boomers have learned to manipulate words through the magic of the word processor.

Reason No. 2 – Defending our Virtue
Secondly, I want to "pass the torch" to the next generation, being sure they don't think we've screwed up everything. Much is wrong with the world of today, but much is positive as well – my way of saying the glass is at least half full. The world is poised at a major tipping point – one way, a path of degradation, the other of potential renovation and renewal. I'm betting on the latter;

Reason No. 3 – Emerging Wisdom
Third, as an emerging elder, I want to share some wisdom with the next generations, let's say those born between 1965 and 2000. Living in the past seven decades, from the 1940s

1

into the decade of 2010, those of my age cohort have learned a great deal about life. Some of our life experiences may be an aide to younger generations;

Reason No.4 – A Lasting Legacy

And lastly, I like to think of my generation, the Baby Boomers, as creative. This is to say, we will leave behind durable additions to history, science, art, and culture.

Notes: *What reasons would you enumerate?*

_____
_____
_____
_____
_____
_____
_____
_____
_____
_____
_____
_____
_____
_____
_____
_____
_____
_____
_____
_____
_____
_____
_____
_____
_____
_____
_____

The First Reason for Writing – Because we can

For many Boomers, writing with clarity, brevity, and with content is a job requirement. For those like me, who worked many years as an administrator of one sort or another, our work required good communication skills. But whether we labor in administrative, technical, or supportive roles, the organizations that employ college trained professionals usually are keen on good written, as well as, verbal skills.

Such skills were often not as necessary for our parents, many of whom worked with their hands more than their minds, and many of whom having endured the Great Depression, did not have the good fortune to complete a college degree. A very special case occurs when someone works as a craftsman, and also enjoys writing. I've often thought I would like to have been an artist, or a sculptor. Others who work with their hands also need a good head to succeed, as in farming and small business, for example.

My dad, Raymond L. Empereur, came from a fairly large family of five siblings all born in the first two decades of the twentieth century. The youngest of five, dad was born in 1919. His father, my grandfather, Marshall Empereur, was an immigrant, arriving here with his parents and other siblings as a young boy from France in 1891.

Marshall never completed much formal education in the north central woodlands of Wisconsin. Education notwithstanding, my grandfather always had work. First he worked in the lumbering industry of northern Wisconsin, then as a railroad line foreman in far off North Dakota, and finally in a foundry in Beloit, Wisconsin, from where he finally retired at age 65 just after the end of World War II.

As far as I can tell, he never became truly literate, and was self educated in the ways of the world. But in his day being lettered mattered little if your work was physical. And

Marshall was a good worker, according to my dad, who also enjoyed robust physical work. And growing up in the Great Depression, dad found work to help boost the family income before graduating from high school, which in fact he never finished.

But dad and mother found success and a middle class life in the world of self-employed small business. Success, by 1956, made it possible to buy the family a new house and a new car. The business, E and B Window Cleaners, prospered and is still in operation today, with my younger brother Mickey and a partner each earning a fair living by specializing in cleaning residential windows.

Grandfather Marshall always admonished his grandchildren to get the best education possible, so that we would not need to rely on strong arms and backs to make a living. The message took, and I became the first in the family to aspire to college, eventually earning both a B.A. and an M.A. I then spent a career in public administration, both in state and local government, eventually settling in to work for several county public health agencies over a span of twenty years.

I've also done some teaching, usually as a part-time adjunct faculty member at several colleges that specialize in degree completion for working adults.

A lot of my contemporaries write as part of their work-a-day lives. Usually, though, it's done in the context of the technical or professional roles we play, in return for our daily bread. For many Boomers, our jobs have required us to write.

The differences between writing to earn a living and writing for pleasure are in form, content, and style. At work, the consumers of our writings are most likely to be a few superiors, subordinates, and colleagues. And, we are no doubt the first generation whose work has been largely

4

transformed from "body" work to "mind" work as my former boss and colleague Dale would say.

We no longer earn a living with our hands, as do farmers or mechanics. Increasingly we work on the tasks that our new, post World War II, service oriented "post industrial" economy demand. These are mind oriented tasks that require cognitive ability more that physical agility. And we must be good at effective use of the written word, as well.

Thus millions of us have come to know one of the most revolutionary tools of the last quarter of the twentieth century... the Boomer invented personal computer. Equipped with powerful Boomer perfected word processing software, these electronic marvels demand increasing amounts of our attention, at work, and for many of us at home and on the Internet, another Boomer invention.

Our generation was the first to make widespread "personal" use of the personal computer, the ubiquitous "PC". And we're the first to use the computer for leisure play. Our kids have quickly mastered the PC too, and today our grandchildren begin using computers by age three!

The first answer to the question, "why write this book?" is simply that having learned to write through college training and mastery of the word processing tool, provides us the means of self expression through the written word.

As for the quality of the effort, you be the judge.

Notes: *Your space for reflection...*

_____

_____

_____

_____

_____

_____

_____

_____

_____

_____

_____

_____

_____

_____

_____

_____

_____

_____

_____

_____

_____

Passing the Torch – Reason Two

There are other reasons, to be sure, for leaving a written record. Among them is to share a bit of personal reflection that others in my generation, and our children and grandchildren, may recognize and value.

That is to say, having lived over parts of seven decades imparts a certain "wisdom" which may be worthy of capturing and imparting to those who will follow. Here, I suppose, is a thinly veiled need to say that my generation has done **some** things right.

We have some values worthy to transmit to our descendants. And we have some insights and a sense of fun about how to enjoy life and find meaning in this crazy world. And, tied up with this need to pass the torch, is the recognition that while youth is still in our vocabularies, so is an emerging awareness of our own mortality, as we enter what some have labeled "the third age".

Thus, self expression through writing is almost therapeutic in making the transition from youth to middle life, and thence onto full maturity. At least it is for me.

What we experience through aging is a natural part of a full and rewarding life. Our parents and grandparents before us learned these same truths. Now, for the first time, many of us born in the post World-War II era also see that we have become the repositories of vast amounts of practical experience imbued with conventional (and unconventional) wisdom.

Let's uncover the light and share some gems of reflective wisdom, for ourselves and our kids. To the word processors, fellow Boomers!!

Notes: Your turn. Describe your writing credentials...

_____
_____
_____
_____
_____
_____
_____
_____
_____
_____
_____
_____
_____
_____
_____
_____
_____
_____
_____
_____
_____
_____
_____
_____
_____
_____
_____

Reason Three – What's It All About?

Don't we take ourselves and our lives too seriously most of
the time? Now don't get me wrong, daily life can be
dreadfully serious! All you need do is watch the evening
news, open your daily newspaper, or listen to the tales of
woe shared at work over the water cooler.

There is much sadness, violence, and hatred in the world. Indeed, these vexations upon mankind seem to be on the increase. And we seem to be increasingly addicted to potentially harmful substances and pleasures of all descriptions, many of which take a self-destructive bent.

Where have we gone wrong? Or, perhaps many of our worst fears are really illusions which are foisted upon us by the mass media, and which we consume and internalize with morbid gusto through the modern magic of instant communication via the radio, TV and now the computer modem or broadband.

In many ways we are both consumers and victims of the media's print and electronic highway.

Certainly, tragedy strikes somewhere everyday. But we needn't live in terror of our neighbor, or of people who are not culturally or racially similar to us, or those who speak a different language, or worship at a different temple, church, or mosque.

Bad things happen everywhere and everyday, but so does much that is positive and good. Intuitively, we all know this. Yet we often dwell morbidly on bad news, presented for us in minute gruesome detail by the electronic and print media.

I wish to emphasize the overwhelmingly positive aspects of human life, and to encourage us toward greater tolerance of human differences. Science tells us that under the skin we're all 99.9% the same, regardless of race.

Let's strive to bring and preserve balance and order to the world, and do it with compassion and good humor. Let's discover the real meaning of life, which a thoughtful friend has defined as simply to "feed the hungry".

Or to paraphrase a wise elder, the great Albert Einstein, who, when asked to comment on the meaning of life, reflected that the meaning of life derives from **serving your fellow man**.

<u>*Notes:*</u> *How did that strike you??*

_____

_____

_____

_____

_____

_____

_____

_____

_____

_____

_____

_____

_____

_____

_____

_____

_____

_____

_____

_____

_____

_____

_____

Reason Four - The Drive for Creativity

Like most everyone, I enjoy a variety of music. From Rock to Jazz and Blue Grass Country, I'm eclectic about music. And I especially like Jazz and classic Rock, since I associate and find comfort with the music of my youth.

I like most of what I hear in contemporary jazz and much of the old tunes too. As a freshman in college, back in '65 at Drake University in Des Moines, I first encountered the jazz of Herbie Mann. I was instantly converted, and still love his many arrangements, my favorite being "Comin Home Baby". Another favorite is the often irreverent Randy Newman. And Sherry and I are fans of The Eagles as well.

I'm also intrigued by the rapid change in the "media" through which popular music has been produced. Since my birth, just a "few" decades back, music reproduction has passed from 78 rpm phonographic records, to 45 rpm to 33 rpm in "stereo" then to reel to reel tape, and on to 8 track tape, to cassette tape, to compact disks and now something called an MP3 player! These days most of us don't even own record players and if we do, they've been packed away or gather dust on some shelf.

Like much in the line of technology, these latter day music reproduction systems have been invented, "created", and perfected by Baby Boomers. We have been a creative generation, like many before us. But unlike previous generations, the pace of invention has increased, quickened, due to new and emerging technology. As a child, I could never have imagined the brave new world that exists today. Nor could I have conceived of so many things we take for granted today, including the wondrous new PC on which I'm composing these words.

Boomers have been creative through many venues. Our jobs have encouraged, if not required, creativity through a drive to become more efficient in the use of time and resources. And creativity may be expressed through many venues, including hobbies such as doing one's own landscaping, or woodworking, or quilting, or gardening, or photography and a myriad of other pursuits.

Being creative is natural and fun. I enjoy writing for fun. What do you enjoy? Be creative, discover your interests, whatever they are, and enjoy the urge to create something uniquely yours.

Notes: *How creative are you??*

_____

_____

_____

_____

_____

_____

_____

_____

_____

_____

_____

_____

_____

_____

_____

_____

_____

_____

_____

_____

_____

_____

Well, how are you doing?

Remember that you are producing notes that you can turn into a lovely document. You may create a personal memoir, to give to your family and for generations of future descendants to glimpse your world...

If only our grandfathers or great grandmothers, or some other long gone member of my family would have left such a record.... How wonderful to hold something produced by one's ancestors. How unique it would be to read their words.

Be as creative with this project as your imagination allows, by inserting photos for example, as I have done. If you have difficulty with the software needed to produce the type of memoir you desire, just ask for help from a son or daughter, many of whom are fully computer literate.

Now, on to my second "essay."

Essay Two: First, Second, and Third Careers

In order that people may be happy in their work, these things
are needed:
They must be fit for it;
They must not do too much of it;
And they must have a sense of success in it.
*John Ruskin, **Pre-Raphaelitism**, 1950.*

Far and away the best prize that life offers
is the chance to work hard at work worth doing.
President Theodore Roosevelt,
September 7, 1903.

He that hath a trade hath an estate;
He that hath a calling hath an office of profit and honor.
*Benjamin Franklin, **The Way to Wealth**, 1757.*

By the time Boomers reach the age of maturity, let's say about "40 something", many have mastered, or at least attempted, more than one vocation or career.

This, I think, sets us apart from most of our parent's generation. There's something in our psyche that harbors or fosters a kind of occupational restlessness. Or, maybe we have what I'll call: The grass is always greener (as in the color of money) syndrome. This, of course, invariably leads many Boomers to move among different careers, perhaps several, over our working lives.

Since we have tended to pursue two or more career paths, logically many Boomers have relocated to different cities or states over time, to take the next rung on the ladder of success. And if children are involved, a move can be extremely traumatic. Kids are usually intolerant of being uprooted from familiar faces and places. They thrive on stability and stress out at major changes in geography. Even a change in school districts can produce a serious backlash from our kids.

Many of my friends and colleagues have experienced career moves. Likewise, my career exemplified this tendency. In the past thirty-five years I've subjected myself and my family to five major career changes, and in the process moved around northern Illinois four times in pursuit of the next "best" career choice.

We have lived in no fewer than eleven different apartments or homes over our married life since 1966. In my two major careers I've held at least twelve different job titles since 1970!

In my third career, that of part-time college teaching, I've taught intermittently for six colleges or universities. My fourth "career", as a non-profit agency director, lasted seven years.

My current and final career (I hope) is that of a self employed health and human services consultant, augmented by part-time work for the University of Illinois, College of Medicine, doing health systems research.

Yet for all this relocating, I have been fortunate in never having been laid off. Perhaps it's been skill, but most likely dumb luck has played a hand as well.

Am I an atypical Boomer? I think not. In all my moves I have experienced some personal and career growth and enrichment. I've been fortunate too, in that most of this occupational risk-taking has led to a gradual and sometime dramatic growth in income. For a career public sector manager my income growth has been significant.

My spouse, Sherry, and I have lived a pretty comfortable middle class existence, and we've managed to put some funds away for our rapidly approaching "golden" years of retirement.

Actually money has always been secondary to the personal satisfaction I felt in my work as a public sector administrator. I never embraced the counter culture of the 1960s, but I did admire their form of rebellion against the status quo, through a motif of love, set in the trappings of rejection of traditional values and capitalism.

Happiness in one's work is far more important than earning a large salary. I took exception to the Yuppie materialistic culture, and always have.

What has been important to me has been having work that in some way contributes to bettering the human condition. But, if your daily labors don't contribute to that goal you can always express your humanity through volunteerism. Boomers have been especially generous with their money and their time…. Volunteering has been a Boomer virtue.

Along the way, Sherry, my spouse and life partner, nurtured our family of four, then took training to become a certified nurse's aid, and for many years has worked in the long term care industry, delivering personal patient care for low wages, and loving her work.

Working with those who are frail and elderly is physically and emotionally challenging, and only special people stay with this work. Working for low wages, she performs work that is necessary to the care of the elderly, who often are disabled with physical ailments or with developing dementia.

It's ironic, and a meaningful social comment, that we so meagerly reward people for providing essential services to the elderly, while sports and entertainment figures are often paid outrageous sums of money.

It was Mother Teresa, I believe who said, *"In this life we cannot do great things. We can only do small things with great love."*

For most of us, "greatness" resides in the eyes of our families, our friends, and in a small circle of colleagues with whom we interact in an amazing variety of career, vocational, professional, or volunteer pursuits.

Success is best measured in terms of a life well lived, by courage and integrity, and through holding on to principles and core values.

Boomers have chalked up more than a little greatness through learning every day to cope with the demands of work, home, and community. Sometimes we've failed. But mostly we've grown into winners, facing challenges and opportunity over the long haul.

As a definition of success, I think that's enough.

Your Turn. What can you say about your career? Make some notes. Define success in your own way...

_____
_____
_____
_____
_____
_____
_____
_____
_____
_____
_____

Raymond W Empereur

_____
_____
_____
_____
_____
_____
_____
_____
_____
_____
_____
_____
_____
_____
_____
_____
_____
_____
_____
_____
_____
_____
_____
_____
_____
_____
_____
_____

Coming up, home ownership.

Essay Three: Our Homes

A man's house is his castle.
Sir Edward Coke, **Institutes,** *vol. III, 1644*

A man builds a fine house; and now he has a master, and a task for life; he is to furnish, watch, show it, and keep it in repair the rest of his days.
Ralph Waldo Emerson, **Society and Solitude: Works and Days,** *1870*

Taxes, after all, are the dues that we pay for the privilege of membership in an organized society. President Franklin D. Roosevelt, October 21, 1936

Perhaps no other group in history has been as successful in the acquisition of real estate as those of us born between 1946 and 1964 – the Baby Boom generation.

Folks born after 1964, the post-Boomers, have yet to demonstrate the economic prowess of the formidable 77 million Boomers. And some Boomers own not one home, but two, or even more. The second is usually in the form of a summer or vacation home or condo.

I admit to having thoughts of a little cottage somewhere, to escape to a lake, or to the mountains. But in reality I don't want all the extra work involved in maintaining more than one residence. And too, I don't need another mortgage. My wanderlust has been satisfied by investing in a little travel trailer, purchased used for 2 grand.

Since 1976, when in our tenth year of marriage and with the financial help of my parents, we mustered enough cash to make the down payment on our first home, we have "owned" five houses in different communities as we have relocated across northern Illinois in a series of career moves.

Each of our homes has been progressively more expensive, not necessarily due to size and amenities, but more owing to the location in proximity to the Chicago area and in general because real estate appreciates over time.

Our first home was purchased in the Rockford, Illinois area for $33,000. That was a nearly new house in 1976 and it felt like a mansion with a half acre lot and attached two car garage.

A few years later in 1983 we moved to Sterling, Illinois where I served as the county public health administrator. Here we purchased our largest house, a 3,000 sq. ft. quad level on nearly and acre for $70,000.

In 1987 came another career move to suburban Will County, near Chicago, where I served as executive director of the county health department. By then, we had acquired three horses, so we bought a rural horse property on 5 acres for $90,000.

In 1991 came another move, this time to McHenry County, another collar county northwest of Chicago, and another horse property on 5.9 acres for $136,000. I worked for the Lake County Health Department in Waukegan, on Lake Michigan and thus had a 43 mile commute each morning.

By 2005, I had taken early retirement from Lake County Health Department, had landed a new job in Rockford, and was commuting 33 miles each morning from Harvard, Illinois. That summer, we purchased our fifth home on the western outskirts of Rockford. This was another horse property on 6.6 acres, purchased for $195,000 and my daily commute was reduced to just 14 miles, round trip.

Ownership, of course, is largely a myth unless you pay cash. The mortgage holder really "owns" the place, and we have the privilege of making payments with interest over a long span of time, usually 30 years. I have never actually owned a home, and frankly don't care to for the simple reason that the IRS allows you to deduct all that mortgage interest! And you deduct those county real estate taxes also.

For many Boomers our homes are our principal source of equity savings. So it pays to take good care of your "investment" by way of making home improvements, such as painting, having new carpet installed, new windows and doors, rain gutters, roofs, creating basement family rooms, etc.

I've long been an inveterate do-it-yourselfer – probably another defining characteristic of Boomers. Some in our age cohort will attempt just about any kind of home improvement. I know I have.

Let's see what home improvement projects have I attempted:
Plumbing,
Carpentry,
Room Additions,
Deck Construction,
Fence Building,
Electrical upgrades,
Heating improvements,
Roofing,
Various floor coverings,
Chimney installation,
Pool installation (and demolition),
Window shades and mini-blinds,
Wall papering,
Installing window air conditioners, humidifiers, de-humidifiers, transfer fans, mercury vapor lights, garage door openers, at least 10 ceiling fans, sump pumps, TV antennas, tier lighting, a satellite dish, and one large awning!

Back in the '80s, we (my wife and kids helped too) built and wired a 24 x 36 pole barn for our horses, complete with an overhead garage door.

I managed to do all these home improvements without having a single "shop" class in school. I know that many Boomers have become accomplished in a wide variety of home projects.

While we take tremendous pride in our homes, we're often frustrated by the labor required for proper upkeep. Thus we may be said to have a love-hate relationship with our real estate holdings. The idea of home ownership is more appealing than the reality, especially at tax time.

Actually, I think real estate taxes are a bad deal for the local governments which impose them. These taxes are costly to administer because of the need to periodically re-assess the value. Real estate taxes are fairly inelastic with regard to growing enough revenue to support the myriad of things that local governments do – from education to animal control to garbage collection, etc. And, of course, real estate taxes are immensely unpopular with the electorate.

Empty nesters, including increasing numbers of Boomers, are not pleased paying for services they no longer use, such as new schools and more teachers. And of course, real estate tax bills (at least in Illinois) arrive just as summer begins, draining you of resources that might have paid for a nice vacation, or that summertime home improvement project!

Here's another theory about why Boomer men and some women like to perform manual labor at home. Many, if not most of us, make our livings doing "mind" work. You know, if you work with paper, telephones, computers, and attend endless meetings, and spend hours at a desk, you grow weary of mind work. Doing something with hand tools feels great!

It's therapeutic to come home and "fix" something. For men, such work restores egos and connects us with our primal roles as hunters and providers. Repairing one's castle conjures the image of the ancient warrior, defending home and hearth. This may sound like baloney; for men it's probably more a function of testosterone.

My theory about mind versus body work may have validity. My dad was a self-employed small business owner, who performed physical "body" work his entire working life, yet he was never compelled to become "Mr. Fixit" at home.

He never fixed a faucet....He called a plumber. I never saw him install an electric outlet or replace a light switch..... Don't electricians do that? As far as painting goes, he usually found a painter to do the task. As small business owners, my parents shared the "mind" work required to keep the business humming, preparing invoices and making payroll. They didn't need the validation we Boomers crave, and receive, through making home repairs.

Seems to me that our need to demonstrate proficiency with tools grows also from our need to connect with our "roots." That is to connect with our fore bearers who mostly had to work with tools on the farm or in the factory. "Mind" work was reserved to a small elite class back in the 19th and early 20th centuries before the rise of the great middle class.

Boomer's interest in home projects has been good for the economy too, giving rise to numerous purveyors of tools and do-it-yourself supplies and commodities. Witness the rise of Menards Home Improvement Centers, Lowes, Home Depot, and other box stores that seem to cater to our passion for fixing and upgrading and making improvements.

Heck, I've been a card carrying member of the "Craftsman Club" at Sears.

Enough said.

Your turn. What feelings, stories, and anecdotes can you conjure up about home ownership? Make some notes here:

_____

_____

_____

_____

_____

_____

_____

_____

_____

_____

_____

_____

_____

_____

_____

_____

_____

_____

_____

_____

_____

_____

_____

_____

_____

_____

_____

Next, we'll move onto another topic that most Boomer families can relate to, our animal companions.

She grew to fear no creature, even our dogs and cat kept their distance from this feisty lady sparrow, as did Indy, a male Indian Ring neck Parakeet that I was given one Christmas.

His full name was Indiana Jones, and eventually he learned to talk a bit, saying "hello" and "thank you". Sherry later acquired a female Cockatiel, that we named Cokie Lemondrop Lowry (don't ask me why). She became more affectionate and talkative than Indy. We eventually sold both exotic birds, but kept BJ until the end of her life.

Sherry has never stopped trying to rescue orphaned baby birds. She did mange to save, raise, and release another sparrow that did fly off when released.

Earlier, I alluded to horses. While we no longer have them, we did keep a variety of saddle horses for a quarter century, and very much enjoyed riding as a hobby. We also became interested in Civil War reenacting, and combined this with our love of horses, and joined a cavalry unit, the 8th Illinois Regiment of Volunteer Cavalry. Over the span of 25 years we owned several horses, and also bought our daughter, Marci, her first horse, which she still has.

So, do you have a personal history with pets? If so make some notes that you can frame into a family story of your own...

_____

_____

_____

_____

_____

_____

_____

_____

_____

_____

_____
_____
_____
_____
_____
_____
_____
_____
_____
_____
_____
_____
_____
_____
_____
_____
_____
_____
_____
_____
_____
_____
_____
_____
_____
_____
_____
_____
_____

Let's consider our spiritual side…

Essay Five: Spiritual Journey

The most acceptable service of God is doing of good to man...
*Benjamin Franklin, **Autobiography**, 1784.*

We have just religion enough to make us hate,
But not enough to make us love one another.
*Jonathan Swift, **Miscellanies**, 1711.*

Going to church doesn't make a man a Christian
Any more than going to a garage makes him an automobile.
Billy Sunday, circa 1920.

An honest God is the noblest work of man.
*Robert G. Ingersoll, **The Gods**, 1872.*

I believe in an America.... Where religious intolerance will someday end –
Where all men and all churches are treated as equal –
Where every man has the same right to attend or not to attend the church of his choice...
Senator John F. Kennedy, September 12, 1960.

The two words that form the title of this essay have been selected to embody what many in our generation perceive to be the "ultimate reality". But what of these two words as concepts?

The concept of life as a "journey" through time has always intrigued me as a fitting metaphor. This is especially true for Boomers who seem to live to travel and often travel to live, (our daily commute to someplace or other). And for us youth oriented middle-agers, a journey is more palatable to contemplate than is the concept of growing old! So let us journey through life, forever young!

Spirituality, on the other hand, may have a different and complex meaning for people of any age, not just Boomers who are approaching, entering, or who are in the full bloom of middle age. For most of us between the ages of 45 and 62, however, spirituality is intrinsically linked with how we view, think about, and participate in organized religion.

The religions of the world have always produced a major influence on the thinking and behavior of the masses. It seems that in western Judeo-Christian culture, from where most Boomers spring, we have become either a part of some large religious tradition imparted to us by our parents, family, or community. Or we have been separated from such traditions through our upbringing, by our parents, or by our own reaction to the confusion, contradictions, and immorality of modern life.

Boomers, I suspect, are also the first generation of modern American history to have seriously questioned traditional religious beliefs at some time during our youth, only to have returned in large numbers to established religion by our middle years. We reclaimed our "family values", including those about spirituality. And for many, belonging to one of thousands of Christian or Jewish faith communities has become a priority.

In our youth, we Boomers experienced social protest movements common in the 1960s. We protested capitalism, consumerism, and American imperialism. We railed against the status quo, against Madison Avenue, against the Military-Industrial Complex, against conformity.

Remember the "God is Dead" movement, the Beat Generation, Flower Children, Existentialism, protesting the war in Vietnam? These were all part of the alienation that many felt toward the mindless pursuit of traditional American capitalistic values. In my late teens and early twenties I identified with the protest movement and became alienated from traditional religious values, becoming what may be described as a secular humanist.

As the first generation raised under the threat of nuclear annihilation, many Boomers challenged tradition in social, political, and religious norms. For some, working in the civil rights movement became a way to express our dissatisfaction with the status quo. Most of us came from white middle class families, the very social group that tolerated racial segregation and bigotry.

Nonetheless, I believe that our generation has taken on the mantle of leadership in slowly reversing out of date views, for example, about race in America. Much has changed since 1964. Finally, white American Boomers made possible the candidacy of Barack Obama, our first African-American President. While not perfect, we are making progress toward a just, color-blind society.

The blatant trappings of 1950s southern racial segregation are long gone, as is much of the more subtle racism practiced in the north, but in large measure the races are still separate. Black Americans are too often unable to participate fully in the dominant white culture. Blacks, and now increasingly Hispanics, are disproportionately represented among the low income, the uneducated, the disenfranchised, those in poor health, and those victimized by crime, drug abuse, and living in dysfunctional families.

This is true in spite of hundreds of examples of Black and Hispanic Americans who have excelled and achieved national prominence in all segments of society, including education, politics, medicine, business, and religion. Still much is left undone in creating a truly just American society, and we must continue to seek the prize.

I am, and have been, an unabashed white middle-class liberal. I do my part in working for a truly just society and urge both Boomers and post Boomers to take up the mantle and continue the work for social justice and racial harmony.

Perhaps our kids and theirs are benefiting from the spiritual struggles of my generation, waged over ethics and morality. Perhaps the true answers to real harmony and shared progress between peoples of all colors, origins, and creeds, lies in strengthening our spiritual foundations, and teaching people that an intact family, living in a sustainable community, is the best place to nurture the spirit.

In our youth, Sherry and I provided a stable, loving home to our kids. We have been very proud of our children as they have become adults and parents in their own right. And right or wrong, we left religion to them, since we did not join any church during their formative years. Our kids have been free to find their own spiritual values.

As for my wife Sherry, she has become an active Christian, while I have found meaning in Unitarian-Universalism. Thus I no longer cling religiously to secular humanism, though I still count my self a humanist.

Sherry has found peace, strength, and true happiness in her Christian beliefs. She strives to live her life in the image of Christ. She has also discovered a whole universe of people who share her convictions.

I have been a Unitarian since 1987. I practice my faith through integrity and honesty in my life and work. As a Unitarian I have the obligation to develop my own theology.

I have come to value all ethical religious traditions which honor the dignity and worth of the human spirit. I strive to be humane and accepting of all people of good will, regardless of color, creed, or sexual orientation.

Thus, I have found religious faith outside of traditional Christianity. And I urge everyone to find a belief system that makes sense to you.

Doubtless most Boomers have different religious values and honor different traditions than mine. I'm happy with that.

We all need to value what gives us nurture and strength.

Your turn: How do you express your own spiritual journey? Make some notes....

_____

_____
_____
_____
_____
_____
_____
_____
_____
_____
_____
_____
_____
_____
_____
_____
_____
_____
_____
_____

How have you been mentored, and how do you mentor?

Essay Six: On Mentoring

You send your child to a schoolmaster, but tis the schoolboys who educate him.
Ralph Waldo Emerson, ***The Conduct of Life: Culture,*** *1860*

The young are often accused of being thoughtless, rash, and unwilling to be advised.
William A. Alcott, ***The Young Man's Guide,*** *1849*

I consider myself to be a pretty average guy. Just a basic solid middle class citizen, who works for a living, plays by the rules, as they say, and pays his taxes without much complaint. I'm average with one exception. I'm not a fan of professional sports, or of NASCAR, and would rather spend spare time writing in my journal, reading, civil war reenacting, camping, hiking, biking, or completing yet another home improvement project.

I also consider myself to have achieved success in life. I've had great careers in public health, in private non-profit management, and now in working for myself. Sherry and I have made a long-term stable loving marriage. Together, we've managed to raise two great children to adulthood, without too many bumps in the road. We have five handsome or beautiful and intelligent (of course) grandchildren. I could go on, but I've made my point. That is, much of my success I attribute to my family.

I believe that we all have a modicum of greatness within, if we pause to consider our achievements; and we have far more potential than most of us will ever tap. How is this so? What well of strength and wisdom do we access that sets us on the correct course to success in life?

I contend that good things in life are not chance events. Rather, good things are achieved through developing a vision of the future and steadfastly pursuing your vision. For men, especially, these concepts are readily embodied in how we think about our careers, our life's work. If we are content in our work, we have a greater prospect to be content in our personal lives as well.

Early in my career, I was mentored by a boss, now my friend Joe, who did his best to impress on me that in his view nothing mattered more that one's career. My boss was a member of the generation born and raised during the Great Depression. That experience, I think, taught him valuable lessons about deprivation, and colored his life perspective significantly. I can recall several discussions with a young woman health professional who worked for the organization. At that time I was second in command, and my boss was the long standing CEO, and a health professional by training. Our young woman, a Boomer like me, had recently completed dental school, and we were her first employer.

The young dentist was single, and her family lived more than a hundred miles away. She missed them terribly and traveled home each week-end. She also had a male friend, who eventually became her fiancé, and he also lived back home. To her, her life's goal was not about career, but rather a quest for happiness which to her meant marriage and a family of her own. Her inattention to her potential career in public health dentistry was a point of some considerable concern to our boss, as well as to one of our board members, himself a dentist and one who had helped recruit this young professional.

To their mature male perspective, the only smart thing for the young woman with professional training to consider was a long term commitment to building a solid career. The young dentist stayed with us but a year. She then returned home, married, and I believe dropped out of the full time practice of dentistry to raise a family.

In both cases, personal goals, while different, were achieved. My former boss had a full career and raised a family as well, with the help of his wife, who put her nursing career on hold to be a stay at home mom. He has been one of my mentors, having been the person who gave me my first job out of graduate school, and started me on the path to my own career in public health. Joe had faith in me, something we all need and are lucky if we find.

Joe introduced me to the field of public health administration at the local level. For five years he taught me his craft, and then he encouraged me to try it on my own. I stayed with that career for twenty years, and was well satisfied with it.

Is there a lesson? I think we are at our best when we are nurturing younger subordinates, training them and helping them to grow and develop in their skills. This is much the same role we take as parents. I know that I was mentored, and like to think that I mentored a few younger colleagues throughout my career.

There's a second lesson, too. Don't make the mistake of allowing your job to dominate your life, especially at the exclusion of family. To be whole, complete, and sane we need a broader focus, I think, to find fulfillment in more than one course in life.

Mentors are at work outside the workplace, in the community. We should strive to be community mentors as well, through the institutions common to all: the church, the schools, social and service organizations and clubs, and within the political structure. Mentoring opportunities abound, and many could benefit from our experience.

Being a mentor carries certain responsibilities and requires certain credentials. Boomers are well suited to the role. We have abundant life experience. Be a force for good and help grow the next generation of leaders.

A mentor is someone who has earned respect; someone who has the wisdom of experience, and the ability to impart that wisdom in a way that instructs without being critical or judgmental.

And mentoring is really a form of teaching, of imparting knowledge about how the world and organizations work. Mentoring is something Boomers have earned the right to practice. More than that, we have the obligation to be mentors to those who follow us in leading the world to a more secure, peaceful future.

OK, your turn. How have you been a mentor? What legacy are you going to leave? Jot down some notes, and formulate your own perspective on how mentoring has touched you....

_____

_____

_____

_____

_____

_____

_____

_____

_____

_____

_____

_____

_____

_____

_____

_____

_____

_____

_____

_____

_____

_____

_____

_____

_____

_____

_____

_____

_____

_____

_____

_____

_____

_____

_____

_____

_____

_____

_____

_____

_____

_____

_____

_____

_____

_____

_____

Time for a change of pace. Let's consider how Boomer families spend time on vacation.

Essay Seven: Family Vacations

"See the U.S.A. in your Chevrolet,
America is asking you to call..."

General Motors jingle, circa 1960
As Sung by Dinah Shore

Dr. Benjamin Spock was the guru of popular wisdom on child rearing for the parents of the first wave of Baby Boomers. His first book, published in 1946, became an instant best seller among the wave of new parents who appeared by the millions in the first few years following the establishment of world peace at the end of World War II. With the war over, millions of ex-GIs were anxious to pick up where they had left off when they deferred their lives to end the Axis dream of world domination.

The World War also ended the Great Depression. And the parents of the Boomer Generation, who themselves have been called the "Greatest Generation" in a book by Tom Brokaw, were to experience the greatest streak of American prosperity in our nation's history. Between 1946 and 1964 the birth rate soared, creating a huge generation of 77 million who were raised in a brave new world of prosperity and consumerism.

Aided by Dr. Spock, our parents raised a great new middle class cradled in relaxed discipline and allowed to grow and experience life guided by loving, nurturing parents. At least many of us were raised free from the harsh discipline advanced by previous generations. In my family there were four siblings, and three of us are Boomers.

During the War, dad served in the Navy, while mom stayed home with their oldest daughter, my big sister Sandra, born in 1942, and worked part time in a defense plant to aid the war effort.

My parents had married in 1939, at the age of nineteen, while the Depression was still a stark reality. They lived modestly until the end of the war brought greater prosperity and my dad, home from the war, started a small business to support his growing family. I was born in 1947 and my younger sister in 1950. Our youngest brother arrived in 1956.

For most Americans, the 1950s brought prosperity, and home ownership soared. Dad and mother purchased our first family home in 1956. The 50's also brought pressure for social change, especially in how society treated people of color, the elderly, and the poor.

The Civil Rights Movement fermented in the 50's and exploded in the 60's, culminating in the Great Society Programs, the Voting Rights Act, and Medicare/Medicaid.

My dad and Uncle Ralph, mom's brother, launched a new business in 1956. They worked hard, and with mother staffing the home office, the business prospered. Mom kept house, cooked, and also learned bookkeeping and small business management. Women's roles were changing and mom was one of the change agents. She had a key role in the business and its ultimate success.

I recall that dad had purchased a beautiful new 1955 Desoto automobile, which he was forced to sell to help capitalize the business. He and mother took a big risk, but the business immediately prospered and dad bought another new Desoto in '56. Thereafter, dad was able to purchase a new car every three or four years.

It was about that time that the family first enjoyed the luxury of a real vacation. At first, in the early 1950's, we would drive up to northern Wisconsin, near Medford, for long summer jaunts to the family farms owned by two of my uncles, Herman and Viola (Empereur) Baars, and George and Winnifred Empereur. Soon we also began frequenting lovely fishing resorts in the lake area near and on the Flambeau Flowage, near Park Falls and Springstead, Wisconsin.

These were great times during which I got to know my cousins and what life on a farm was like. My dad and uncles loved to fish, and we kids loved being in the great northern Wisconsin woodlands.

Here's a family gathering from that period.

Empereur Family Group c.1954
at Hannibal, WI

Front row (L-R): Eugene, Ray W., Catherine; 2nd Row: Sandra, Ray L., Louisa Mae Baars, Winnie holding daughter Carol, Yvonne holding Jean Suzanne; Back row: Genie and Marshall, with Louise behind Sandra.

Some of my favorite trips were to the fishing resorts in northern Wisconsin, traveling in a two car caravan with Uncle Merlin, dad's other brother, Aunt Marge and their son, Mike. They drove in their Pontiac Chieftain and our family in the four door Desoto.

Merlin and Marge owned a tavern in Afton, a hamlet located between Beloit and Janesville, Wisconsin, about 25 miles from our Loves Park, Illinois home. Since they were very close, we spent lots of time with dad's older brother and his family.

Merlin and Marge loved to fish, so we usually traveled "up north" with them. Dad's other siblings also lived in northern Wisconsin, and we saw them much less frequently- usually only on our summer trips.

So, with our family (Dad, Mom, Sandy, Jean, Mick, and me) in the Desoto, and Merlin, Marge, and son Mike in the Chieftain, we made several trips to northern Wisconsin between 1956 and 1960, a hefty 300 miles to the north woods.

We stayed at neat knotty pine cottages, in quaint fishing resorts like The Birches, on Boot Lake, which had been opened at the end of World War II. There was a main lodge with a massive stone fireplace and many mounted trophy fish, deer, and other creatures. In front of the lodge, at the edge of Boot Lake, was a pier and swimming beach, where we spent many summer afternoons.

Some day's, cousin Mike and I would accompany our dads on a fishing excursion. We fished for anything that would bite, usually perch, crappies, walleyes, or bullheads. Dad would always let me run the motor. It was a temperamental Firestone 4 horse which never ran as smooth or as fast as Uncle Mer's 5 horse Johnson.

I always envied the guys with the bigger, faster outboards. If we could only get a 10 horse we could fly across the lake! But we never did.

I'm pleased that the Birches is still in business and is still owned by the same family. In recent years I've accompanied my dad and brother Mick on several summer fishing trips. More recently my son, son-in-law, and their boys have also journeyed with us to Boot Lake.

At The Birches Resort, c. 1960

By 1960 my folks tired of the annual summer trips up north, and with the centennial of the Civil War, dad became enamored with visiting the major battlefields and learning all he could about that great and terrible conflict. And he wanted his kids to learn about American history as well.

Thus, in the summer of 1960, we began a series of summer odysseys in a new Chrysler Saratoga. Every year through 1966, we spent up to four weeks each summer visiting various parts of the country, the East, South, and West.

In '64, we traveled in a new Chrysler New Yorker. This time dad bought one with air conditioning! During these summer excursions we even took in parts of Canada. And in '65, we drove a new Dodge van all the way to Mexico City and back. We had become a two car family.

Dad became a Civil War buff during the centennial, so in the early '60s we visited nearly every major battlefield or historic site – from Bull Run to Ft. Sumter; from Gettysburg to Appomattox; from Vicksburg to Chickamauga.

While in the Deep South, we were exposed to the ugliness of racial segregation during its final formal years. We lived in a "lily white" northern suburb, and this was the first time I had ever seen large numbers of black people. I was both impressed and appalled with the abject poverty we observed among Blacks in the rural South.

In Mississippi, we met some local people who befriended us. They became family friends and dad and mother visited them often in the years that followed. They even came north a few times to visit us. Charles and Francis lived in the land of King Cotton, and Charles managed a modern Cotton Gin. How different their ways and customs seemed.

We also traveled out West, to the Badlands, Deadwood, Wall Drug, the Corn Palace, Yellowstone, and the Grand Canyon. One year we were in California and Washington State, then on to Vancouver Island in British Columbia.

On one trip out East we took in D.C., Boston, and NewYork City, even attending a New York Yankees home game. Dad adored his Yankees, which was somewhat odd for a Midwesterner in the land of the Cubs, Milwaukee Braves, and White Sox.

In the summer of '65 we spent a month on tour of the Southwest and on to Mexico City. This was the year Sherry and I, then sweethearts, graduated from high school. She and a friend of my sister accompanied us, making a group of seven in all. Dad had a brand new Dodge van and since this was a camping trip, we towed a small rented Apache pop-up camper all the way as well. Even with seven people and all their stuff we managed to have enough room and even enjoyed the trip.

The following summer of 1966, we took the family boat, a small 20 foot cabin cruiser down the Illinois River from Starved Rock to the Mississippi, and then all the way to New Orleans, and returned, with six people on board.

I recall spending a steamy hot July night in Vicksburg, Mississippi. We had tied our boat alongside the Sprague, one of the most famous retired steam powered tow boats of all time. Too hot to sleep, I had spent most of the night exploring that massive old riverboat, walking her several decks on a steamy summer night in Mississippi. She had been build in Dubuque, Iowa during the 1920's, and was the most powerful steam tow boat of her age. Sadly, this floating museum, which was mostly wood above the steel hull, was lost to fire some time later.

In May 1969, I graduated from Rockford College. In August, after 3 years of marriage, Sherry and I welcomed our firstborn son, Chad. By September, my college deferment having expired, I was drafted into the Army. Since I had passed two previous pre-induction physicals, I was certain to be going soldiering, probably to Viet Nam.

In an effort to get the best possible deal from Uncle Sam, I decided to enlist prior to reporting for the draft. A critic of the war in Viet Nam, I was nevertheless not of a mind to escape the draft. I decided that if called, I would serve.

Shortly thereafter, early one September morning, I was packed and on my way to the Chicago Induction Center, with a small cadre of fellow enlistees, mostly kids of 18 or 19. By then, at age 22, I was a college graduate and a new father, and felt like an old man compared to my companions. I sometimes wonder what became of the young men who entered the Army that day.

At dad's urging I carried something else into Chicago that September day. I brought a medical report from my surgeon to explain the long scar I carried on my left elbow. Dad was against the war in Viet Nam, and hoped that the medical report of my damaged elbow would somehow get me rejected, or assigned to a non-combat role. I had my doubts.

My scar had resulted from a serious injury sustained five years earlier as a high school wrestler. I had taken a bad fall and had dislocated the joint, requiring a surgical procedure and several weeks of recovery. I had indeed lost some extension of the left arm, but I had normal function, no pain, and no other limitations that I could detect. Seeing the report and the scar, an army medical examiner pulled me from line, x-rayed my elbow, and pronounced me "medically unfit" for duty. To my surprise and amazement, the Army found my elbow too unstable for military life! By evening, I was back home courtesy of the Army, via a Greyhound bus ticket.

So certain was I that I would be inducted that day, we had moved out of our apartment and Sherry and Chad were to stay with her parents, at least for a while. Luckily, our apartment had not been rented and we were able to move back in within the week! Thus ended my brief military career.

This unexpected turn of events left me determined to find a peaceful way to public service. In July of 1970 I began a seven year career as a rehabilitation counselor and casework supervisor with the Illinois Division of Vocational Rehabilitation. That was followed by 20 years working in administration of several local governmental public health agencies throughout northern Illinois.

Dad and mother were so happy to have me back home that a while later they surprised us with another family trip. This was to be the crowning vacation of the 1960s – a ten day trip to the Hawaiian Islands. We flew from O'Hare after

Christmas and returned in the first week of 1970. Chad, being too small for travel, was left in the care of Sherry's sister, Sandra.

I've always been grateful to my parents for those many summer trips, as well as the winter excursion to Hawaii. I developed a love of travel. Later, mom and dad would travel to exotic places, visiting Australia and New Zealand, as well as the Bahamas, the Dominican Republic, and even a cruise in the Caribbean.

In celebration of their 50th wedding anniversary in 1989, my parents took the whole family, including kids, spouses, and grandkids, 18 in all, to Cancun, Mexico on a ten day trip. Four years later, we all went to Ixtapa, Mexico, on the west coast. Again Mother and Dad hosted. In the years that followed, my parents hosted three family cruises in the Caribbean and another trip to Mexico in 1997, as pictured at the beginning of this book.

Dad and Mother were giving us far more than a monetary inheritance. They gave the family wonderful memories of exotic places. Thanks, mom and dad, for giving the family so many great adventures to remember!

How has your family defined recreation or vacations? First make some notes, and then draft your own story.

_____
_____
_____
_____
_____
_____
_____
_____
_____

Next, let's consider developing a vision...

Four generations of Empereurs at the Birches on Boot Lake.

Essay Eight: The Vision Thing

*How beautiful is youth! How bright it gleams. With its
illusions, aspirations, dreams!*
Henry Wadsworth Longfellow, "Moritutri Salutamus", 1875

Follow your bliss!
Joseph Campbell

Success in life requires each of us to form and pursue a
vision for the future. Our visions are, if managed well,
transformed into goals, and a general plan to reach our goals
results.

As a youth, my future vision was strongly influenced by
sitting at the knee of my grandfather, Martial Joseph
Empereur. He was 66 when I arrived in January, 1947. He
had already far exceeded the life expectancy for people born
in the latter half of the 19th century. My memories of
Grandpa Empereur are of a kindly old man who, as he would
say, thought "the world and all" of his many grandchildren.
Frequently, he would admonish me to become educated, as if
it were the most important thing in the world. To him little
else seemed important.

It was later, at his death at age 85, that I realized that this
gentle French born patriarch had never completed any real
formal education. He arrived in northern Wisconsin in 1891,
as a boy of nine, with his parents and six siblings. Through
hard work, the family established a farm in rural northeast
Wisconsin, near the village of Marion. There was little time
for school.

Two years later in 1893, his mother died, and in 1895, his
father died as well, leaving the family in the care of the
oldest son, Joseph Cyprien, who was then 26. Frank Sr., as

he came to be known, worked hard to keep the family of seven siblings together, running the farm to generate the income needed to support the family. Sometimes he would hire-out his younger siblings to the neighbors. Times were tough and two of the seven were dead by 1898; Marie, age 16, of illness and Joseph Achille, "Archie", age 21, to a train accident.

Martial, just 14 when his father suddenly died, disliked farming and the rigid rules imposed by his oldest brother. He left home as soon as he could, probably before age 18, to find his own way, and sadly never had time for much school.

Grandfather had worked hard during his life, but his lack of education limited his choices. Barely able to sign his name, my paternal grandfather never learned to read well if at all, and thus his occupational choices were seriously limited. During his life, Martial farmed, lumber jacked, worked as a section foreman on the rail road in North Dakota, and finally ended his working life in a Beloit, Wisconsin foundry.

He and Grandmother Genie lived modestly, and managed to raise five children, have a successful marriage, and survived the Great Depression. Grandfather was nearly illiterate, and while he worked hard to support his family, never knew the simple joy of reading a book. Nor did he ever obtain a driver's license. From descriptions of grandfather provided by my older cousins, he also probably suffered from episodes of chronic depression as well.

When I entered college at Drake University in the fall of 1965, I realized the visions of two people. I became the first in the family to attend college, and in doing so fulfilled a promise made to my grandfather, and a vision of success for myself.

I have come to believe that the defining difference between people who are hopeful and enthusiastic for life, and those who lack direction, is their ability to form a vision of the future and to develop and pursue personal goals with success. Having a future vision has a lot to do with how one achieves a sense of personal worth and competence as well.

Martial Joseph and Genie Empereur (circa 1960)

By now, Boomers are fairly good at the "vision thing"; or we should be, having lived long enough to have formed and pursued several. Most of us have by now achieved more than one personal goal. I know I have.

My first occupational goal was to become a teacher and I felt my destiny was to use college to prepare for a career in education. I now realize that many young people consider being teachers, as it is the one profession that they experience first hand as children.

Mr. Martin, my high school history teacher, embodied what I wanted to become. Poised, confident, articulate, he had a passion for his craft, and made history come alive for us 10th graders at Harlem High School in Loves Park, Illinois.

It was in his class, through the school intercom, that word reached us that President Kennedy had been assassinated in November 1963. Mr. Martin wept openly at the news, as did many of his students. Yes, I wanted to be like Mr. Martin!

My plans for becoming a teacher coincided with the same plans of millions of my fellow Boomers. After high school, I entered Drake University at DesMoines, Iowa, and pursued a BA in history and political science. At the end of my first year, I married my high school sweetheart, and moved home to attend Rockford College, where I could both continue to pursue my degree, and help dad run the family business on a part-time basis, and full time during the summers.

By the time of graduation in May 1969, Sherry and I were preparing for the arrival of our first born, Chad, born that August. I elected to remain at Rockford College to pursue a Master's in Teaching. Two weeks after beginning classes, however, fate and Uncle Sam handed me another plan. I was drafted.

I did not end up in the military. The Army, to my great surprise, found me medically unfit for soldiering due to an old high school sports injury. By the time life returned to normal, I had lost interest in continuing school. With my new B.A., I felt it was time that I turned to the business of working full time to help support my little family.

I began my first quest for employment and entered the job market in the fall of 1969. I reasoned that teaching was not my destiny, and after flirting briefly with the idea of employment in the family business or in life insurance or real estate, I began to focus on careers in the social services. Idealistic, I wanted to somehow contribute to making the world a better place.

My first job quest lasted fully nine months. And, to land a desirable job I had to move the family 150 miles from home to work in Peoria in central Illinois. During all that searching I worked full time in the family business as a window cleaner. Ironically, I was earning more as a window cleaner than that first "professional" position paid. I reported for work on July 1, 1970 as a Social Services Career Trainee for the State of Illinois for an annual salary of $7,500.

That one decision, made nearly 40 years ago, became the defining point of my career. While I've held many jobs of increasing complexity and responsibility over time, and later completed an advance degree in public administration, my primary work has been in the field of managing health and human services.

I even eventually did become a teacher as well. I became part-time adjunct faculty for several colleges, teaching public administration, public health, and health administration.

To my point – sometimes our first plans don't work, and that's alright. You can always make a new plan. In my case, I've made a pretty good career out of my *second* choice.

Boomers have a lot to share with their kids and grandkids about the importance of having and chasing a vision. Sometimes, with hard work and good luck, dreams do come true.

So what can you say about your visions of success? What do you desire to share with your descendants? Make some notes here:

_____
_____
_____
_____
_____
_____
_____
_____
_____
_____
_____
_____
_____
_____
_____
_____
_____
_____
_____
_____
_____
_____
_____

Next, we'll consider things we own.

Essay Nine: Our Possessions

*This is the only country that ever went to the poorhouse
in an automobile.*
Will Rogers, written during the Great Depression

*A man is rich in proportion to the number of things
he can afford to let alone.*
Henry David Thoreau, <u>Walden</u>, 1854

Boomers are masters of consumption. Sometimes it's been conspicuous, at other times just necessities of life. Either way, Boomers have made the retail world go round for many years. We'll buy just about anything, in part because there are just so many of us, over 70 million, that we represent a full range of tastes.

Recently I discovered "The Boomer Project – The Nation's Authority on Today's Boomer Consumer." It's on the World Wide Web, and offers tips on how to market products and services to members of our generation. The site also hosts an on-line newsletter, "Jumpin Jack Flash", by free subscription twice monthly and geared to Boomers over age 50.

We're a diverse group, representing all cultural roots and all ethnic and racial backgrounds. Many of us live a singles life, but many more have married (at least once) and have been busy raising the next generation and even welcoming our first grandchildren to the world.

Perhaps no single possession is as important to a Boomer as his or her "ride". We currently own two, one for her and one for him. Yes, we actually have clear title to both, no car payments, at least for now.

Boomers are in love with our cars, and trucks, and vans, and sport utilities. We say we need them. And many Boomers have been able to afford the luxury of "rapid turn-over" of our vehicles. As a group we buy and sell or trade lots of vehicles. I recently owned a third car, a red convertible, which I recently sold. It was my "middle age crisis" car.

We seem to love all types of vehicles, domestic and imported, large and small. Until recently the low price of gas meant that we could own and love inefficient vehicles, like big 4x4 SUVs and trucks.

I can claim to have owned over 30 different vehicles since 1965, many of them new, and a full variety of cars, trucks, vans, and SUVs as well. I've owned Fords, Chevys, and Chryslers, AMC models, Plymouth, Dodge, Jeep, Nissan VW, and MG versions. Oh, and I've owned one International Scout as well.

My first car was the most memorable, a 1965 Plymouth Barracuda, which mother and dad gifted to me upon graduation from high school as a vehicle to drive to and from Drake University in Des Moines.

The first generation "Cuda", in gleaming copper metallic paint, looked very much like the picture that follows, copied from an original Plymouth brochure. Can you imagine a new car for $2,500? Heck, new and most used, Harley-Davidson Motorcycles cost much more today. We loved that little fastback, which unfortunately was demolished in my first, and only (so far), car wreck in April 1970. By the way, I was not at fault.

Like most guys I love the smell of new upholstery, and the look of new tires, clean bright engines, and fresh gleaming paint. I've also enjoyed looking at cars, and I've looked at and bought many over the years. But besides being bedazzled by the wizards of motor city, what else have Boomers consumed?

For less than $2300*, your new fastback Barracuda comes with 14.4 sq. ft. of fully tinted glass in the rear window—largest of its kind ever put into a standard production car. And that's only one of the many comfort, convenience and style features designed into this car for people of all ages and interests.

1965 Plymouth Barracuda – from an original Chrysler Corp. brochure

Boomers have probably purchased more "stuff" than all other previous American generations combined! Boomers have been mass consumers, including every kind of electronic gadget, clothing fads, new concepts in food or food packaging, and all the latest toys and games.

And to keep age at bay, many have gone under the knife for plastic surgery.

Heck, with my new PC and broadband on line access, I've recently joined Face book. And, with the help of our granddaughters, my wife is now into texting on her cell phone.

As regards our enthusiastic consumerism, every indication is that our kids have learned to imitate our eclectic behavior.

This is truly a victory for the likes of TV's Billy Mays and the product designers and marketing wonks.

Boomers as a class have arrived at a level of financial success that facilitates a high level of surplus consumption. Given the current mega recession, however, our kids, if they seek to emulate our behavior over the long term, will have to wait for the restoration of their income potential.

This begs the question of the morality of conspicuous consumption. At some level we all love our "toys", be they snowmobiles, sports cars, Blackberries, boats, or exotic pets – things that make us happy, or give us pleasure.

Many of us have begun to recognize that happiness does not come from satisfying every fantasy. Having things does not make one happy. It seems that the more we have the more we want... and we have endless wants.

Living as consumers is part of our evolved need to live within communities. Human kind is not self sufficient. To live, we must sell our labor, or the fruits of our labor, to acquire those goods and services that we cannot produce on our own. The buying and selling of goods and services is simply the economic side of social interaction.

Being human is really all about the relationships we develop with our families and fellows. So here's some sound advice to my fellow Boomers and their kids and grandkids: Be consumers. Become good at commerce and getting value for your hard earned dollar. It's important to living successfully in modern society. But don't allow your pursuit of possessions to become the central meaning of your lives.

Some among us have departed from the consumer culture to embrace the concept of "voluntary simplicity." Duane Elgin, author of the book *Voluntary Simplicity,* said: *"Simple living is not about living in poverty or self-inflicted deprivation.*

Rather, it is about living an examined life – one in which you have determined what is important, or "enough," for you, discarding the rest."

Given our emerging priority to reduce our "carbon footprint" in order to sustain a livable natural environment beyond the current century, we all must resolve to reduce our demand for non-essential and resource wasting products.

Think about every purchase in terms of its utility and ultimate end. Is this product needed? How long will it last? What becomes of it when I discard it?

If more of us act in this manner, just maybe we can contribute to the long term survival of the one possession we all must share.....Planet Earth.

How do possessions play in your life?

_____
_____
_____
_____
_____
_____
_____
_____
_____
_____
_____
_____
_____
_____
_____
_____
_____
_____

Raymond W Empereur

_____
_____
_____
_____
_____
_____
_____
_____
_____
_____
_____
_____
_____
_____
_____
_____
_____
_____

How good are you at relationships?

Essay Ten: Relationships

*Back of every achievement is a proud wife
and a surprised mother-in-law.*
Brooks Hays, aide to President Kennedy, December 1, 1961

The family is one of nature's masterpieces.
*George Santayana, **The Life of Reason, Vol. 2, Reason in
Society, 1905***

Boomers are, in the main, relationship junkies. That is to say, as consumers of popular culture and contemporary psychology, we've been captured and captivated by Dr.Phil and numerous other purveyors of success in human interactions.

Real men, mature men, of the Boomer generation are supposed to be sensitive, caring nurturers, not the testosterone laden chauvinists we were born to be. Today's modern man is likely to be as good in the kitchen as in the bedroom. Although there are occasional "throwbacks", that is, men who revert at times to the rutting, strutting behavior typical of previous generations of men.

Many guys of my generation have been active in childrearing and housework, in addition to sharing kitchen chores, as well as becoming fairly adept at communicating with the female of the species. I even became expert at diaper changing, a fact unheard of by men of my father's generation, who saw themselves as the principal breadwinners and not as children's caretakers.

Today, bringing home the bacon is more often a shared venture between "life partners". The fact is that many Boomers have non-traditional families. Two incomes is the norm today, whereas during my childhood, mother was the homemaker, although she too helped with the family business, which my parents ran from our home.

And today, men are actually likely to find themselves reporting to a woman on the job. My first experience with a woman boss came on the first day of my first professional job way back in 1970. She was a tall, mature, meticulous woman of nearly 60. A lifelong professional social worker, Agnes was a Casework Supervisor, for the Illinois Division of Vocational Rehabilitation at the Peoria Regional Office.

Although kind and caring, she appeared stern, with close cropped hair, always impeccably dressed in business attire. In spite of her outward demeanor, this woman won my immediate respect and admiration. Highly professional, she embraced the agency mission. Personal concerns came second. She was a master of both the professional and process sides of social casework, which was, and still is, bound up in paper, forms, and rules. Agnes was my first mentor.

Agnes directed my training and was ably assisted by another single woman, Sue, who was a former Catholic Nun. Sue had been with the agency for about two years, and helped me learn the ropes.

Since that first experience working for and with women, I have worked in a field of endeavor, public health, in which women form at least 70 percent of the workforce. It's true that men still dominate the leadership structure of these public sector organizations, while women make steady gains in crashing through the glass ceiling.

And this is rightfully so, since women are at least the intellectual equals of men, especially in the performance of "mind" work such as in public administration. In the world of the future, I would expect that fully half of all management jobs would be held by smart, capable women.

I've digressed, though I'm certain that my experience in relationships is by no means unique. Thus far, I've touched upon roles and relationships in marriage and work, but what of family and friends?

We choose our friends and some choose us, but we inherit our family. I'm not a gregarious person, and while I have many acquaintances or business associates, I have only a few close friends. In the world of business we must become adept at formal interpersonal skills when communicating with co-workers, be they peers, subordinates, and superiors.

With family, we are placed into close contact with people who we often did not choose. Family relationships are often times more tenuous, and fragile, because invariably at least some family members are people that you would not have chosen as friends.

Friends are ours to enjoy. Friends are people to have fun with, and to trust with exposing your real self, the side of your personhood that you rarely display. Friends are also people to turn to when you need help, and for you to offer help to when needed. This can be, and hopefully is, true for many families as well.

Family can be close, as in your spouse, children and grandchildren, and your siblings and parents. Family can also be relations who we rarely see, or in some cases don't know at all.

Three years ago, I embarked on an effort to connect with members of my extended family. I began collecting names and addresses and phone numbers and e-mail addresses for as many descendants of my French great grandfather, Pierre Maurice Empereur (1844-1895) as possible. I was eventually able to find over 100 relatives, including a dozen or so living in France.

I began The Empereur Family Newsletter, and am this year in the third edition, producing four issues per year. We even re-established annual family reunions, something that my grandparents began in the 1950s, but which stopped occurring due to the deaths of most of my parents' siblings by the mid 1990s.

One of my great aunts, Alma Busker, was an amateur genealogist, and had compiled an impressive history of my paternal grandmother, Genie Pearl Davis's family. Upon Alma's death, I inherited her substantial set of records which trace the Davis side back to one William Seely in 1579, in England.

With the help of Ancestry.com and our newly found French cousins, I now have traced the Empereur family to one Gabriel Empereur-Perret of France, circa 1719.

In the course of my research and in founding a family newsletter, I've met some fine people who also happen to be relatives.

My advice is to enjoy your family and your friends. Hold them close. Life is too short not to share with faithful companions, be they friends or relatives.

So, what have you to say about relationships?

_____

_____

_____

_____

_____

_____

_____

_____

_____

_____

_____

_____

_____

_____

_____

_____

_____

_____

_____

_____

_____

_____

_____

_____

_____

_____

_____

_____

_____

_____

_____

_____

_____

_____

_____

Good. Let's turn now to life long learning.

Essay Eleven: Lifelong Learning

Only the educated are free.
Epictetus, **Discourses**, *1st Century AD*

Learn to live and live to learn.
*Bayard Taylor, "**To My Daughter**" – mid 19th Century*

Like most Americans I enjoy FM radio, especially while driving, and like many Boomers I've come to enjoy listening to public radio. In my case it's WNIJ, Northern Public Radio, which is housed at Northern Illinois University in DeKalb, about 50 miles from my home in Rockford.

I enjoy public radio for its content, for the information and in depth coverage of news as well as the coverage of ideas and issues. I have come to associate public radio with my interest in lifelong learning. Of course I also surf the radio dial for jazz or classic rock, which are my favorite forms of music, but I also learn a great deal from the thoughtful programming available through NPR.

As a group, Boomers have always been interested in learning, and are the best educated class of people in history. Still, many of us have become anxious, especially in the current economic climate, with all the down-sizing, right-sizing, and out-placing of jobs. People age 45 to 62 are worried about being laid-off and becoming chronically unemployed, and thus many of us have been learning new skills in order to keep pace with younger workers, who are more likely to work for less money.

To me, and, I suspect, to a lot of us 45 to 62 year olds, on-going education is natural, fun, and adds to the real joy of living. I have never felt anxious about finding and holding a job. I've been fortunate, never having to face the prospect of long term unemployment. But, having known friends, family, and colleagues who have endured several months without a regular paycheck, I know the wolf may have been only a few short weeks from my door at any time.

In today's world job security is largely an illusion. Virtually every managerial job I've held has been "at will", meaning that my job was on the line from day to day. I worked well under this stress because I was always confident in my ability perform well, and if necessary, to find another position. And this reality helped to stimulate me to keep current with changes in my field of public administration.

Now that I'm semi-retired and work largely as a health and human services consultant, I'm no longer certain that I could find a full-time job to my liking. It's not due to my age; I'm over 60, and I think that older workers are still highly marketable. My fear for my fellow Boomers is that the economy is not currently generating enough jobs for all who seek them.

This fact makes lifelong learning even more important. So, for as long as I live, I plan to continue to learn and to grow intellectually. Another benefit to learning is that when the mind is stimulated we can stall the inevitable decline that aging brings. I hope to be mentally alert until my physical body finally gives out, hopefully many years from now.

In conclusion, my message is simple and self evident. Whatever your age, never lose the thrill that learning a new skill brings. Boomers have embodied this message with great success.

Has life long learning changed you life? How would you share you experiences with your heirs?

_____

_____

_____

_____

_____

_____

_____

_____

_____

_____

_____

_____

_____

_____

_____

_____

_____

_____

_____

_____

_____

_____

_____

_____

_____

_____

_____

_____

_____

_____

_____

Let's turn to recreation. How do you have fun?

Essay Twelve: Fun Times

There can be no high civilization
Where there is not ample leisure.
Rev. *Henry Ward Beecher,* **Proverbs from Plymouth Pulpit,**
1887

He enjoys true leisure who has time
to improve his soul's estate.
Henry David Thoreau, **Journal,** *February 11, 1840*

In itself and in its consequences the life of leisure
Is beautiful and ennobling in all civilized men's eyes.
Thorstein Veblen, **The Theory of the Leisure Class,** *1899*

An essay on having fun seems to be in order, since recreation is an important, if not crucial part of a healthy balanced lifestyle. And by the way, except for the idle rich as first portrayed by Mr. Veblen, we Boomers may be the first generation in the history of the planet to have come of age with the expectation of taking a regular annual vacation, and having enough leisure time and money to enjoy regular recreation and hobbies!

After all, reflecting on the economic and social conditions during the time that our parents were raised, during the 1920s, 30s and 40s, one can readily see why this is true. On the American family farm (which by the way is rapidly vanishing), where many of our parents began their lives, the 1920's was far from a booming time. Then the Great Depression hit in 1929 and carried on until World War II. We Boomers arrived after the war and just in time to be part of the greatest wave of prosperity that the World has yet seen. Our parents could actually afford to take vacations.

We must not confuse the idleness of the Great Depression as leisure time – it was a desperate time for many in America who slipped into poverty in greater numbers than ever before. And during the World War that shocked our economy into full production, thus ending the Depression, we were far too busy with the business of defeating the Axis powers, and helping save the Brits, French, and Russians to enjoy any leisure time.

Down on the farm, most folks didn't even have electricity until the mid to late 1930s, and true mechanized farming was just getting its start. After the war and well into the 1950s, our parents were busing going back to school, working, raising us, and building a new society. Again, there was not much leisure.

I can vividly recall my dad working on his new business venture nearly every Saturday and some Sundays too. He would leave for work in the early morning and not return home till dark. Dad and mother worked long and hard. While dad was away working for the day, mom kept busy doing all the cooking and cleaning and also answered the phone and kept the books for E and B Window Cleaning, while also doing most of the child care for four young children.

As the business prospered, we too began to enjoy the fruits of the American consumer based economy. I recall our first television set arriving sometime in the early 1950s. Now ubiquitous, TV was a novelty during my early childhood.

Having been invented during the 1920s, TV could not be made into a viable industry in an economy racked by the Great Depression. During World War II, no new consumer products could be produced. Following the war it took time to develop the infrastructure necessary to make TV a paying commercial enterprise, including the networks and broadcast facilities. And, of course, it wouldn't become successful until common folks had enough income to purchase such a luxury and become convinced of its worth.

After all, my parents were raised during the golden age of radio and the movies. Radios were plentiful and cheap. Movies, too, had become a mass entertainment medium by the 1940s. Our first television arrived when I was a lad of 7, some time in 1954. It was a new Zenith console model with a 14 inch screen and a picture in beautiful black and white. There were just two channels available in Rockford, received via a small rabbit ear antenna perched atop the console.

Many of the stars of radio and the silver screen made the transition to television, people like Phil Silvers, Bing Crosby, Bob Hope, Ethel Merman, Lucille Ball, Jack Benny, and many more. The picture was small and grainy, and reception wasn't always good, but you could bring your favorite crooner or comedian to your own living room. And, many of the shows were live as well.

Nearly 60 years later we have digital TV obtained through a satellite receiver which brings dozens of cannels, with full color and stereo sound. In order to fully appreciate the changes that have come to television, well, you had to be there when the medium was in its infancy. We Boomers were.

Perhaps in the not too distant future TV will evolve further, maybe projecting three dimensional holographic images into your living room. What sounds like science fiction today, may become reality tomorrow.

Our kids, now well into adulthood, were raised with color TV and many other modern wonders that didn't exist when Boomers first appeared on the scene in 1946. Today's youth could not imagine life without DVDs, microwave ovens, digital cameras, stereo sound, central air conditioning, space flight, super highways, garage door openers, electric can openers, electric blankets, gourmet coffee, frozen dinners, cellular phones, the Personal Computer, the Wii, and many, many more.

These and other marvels of technology have allowed us to fill our leisure time as well as to learn new skills. There is also a whole set of luxury leisure items that some Boomer families have acquired and enjoyed.

These items include stuff like power boats, travel trailers, jet skis, snow mobiles, all terrain vehicles, motorcycles, motor homes, and swimming pools, and were unavailable to most of my parent's generation. These toys are expensive and thus require a significant family income. American Boomers comprise the largest group to ever possess such luxury recreational items.

Boomers are among the most sedentary and most active of generations. Many of us have enjoyed sports and a variety of other athletics. Now with our youth waning, many of us need to slow down a bit. I enjoy cross country skiing in winter and biking in the summer. In my younger days I was a pretty good water skier, but no longer.

Boomers would be well advised to enjoy at least one leisure time activity that involves exercise. Keeping fit is important to longevity and weight control, and you can keep it simple.

Try some vigorous walking several times a week for at least 30 minutes. It's a splendid fitness activity, available at no cost.

But whatever you do, have fun.

Tell us your own story about having fun.

_____
_____
_____
_____
_____
_____
_____
_____
_____
_____
_____
_____
_____
_____
_____
_____
_____
_____
_____
_____
_____
_____
_____
_____
_____
_____

Reading is another inexpensive leisure time activity, and vital to keeping the mind fit as well.

Essay Thirteen: Being Well Read

The chief glory of every people arises from its authors....
Samuel Johnson, *Preface to* **A Dictionary of the English Language**, *1755*

It takes a great deal of history to produce a little literature.
Henry James, **Hawthorne**, *1879*

All literature is yet to be written.
Ralph Waldo Emerson, **Literary Ethics**, *1838*

I'm convinced that Boomers are among the most literate generations in world history. And yet, ironically, I suspect we are not among the best read of generations.

Many of us shun reading books. We devour newspapers and magazines, yet too few of us have discovered, and cultivated the joy of books. It matters not whether you choose fiction, history, detective novels, love stories, or poetry, reading books does broaden our scope and allows us to freely use our imaginations as well. This helps to keep the mind fit and agile.

I've always been a history buff, and own many favorite volumes, which I plan to leave to my heirs. In fact my undergraduate major was U.S. History. My special interest is the history of the American Civil War.

Usually I'm in the midst of reading one or two volumes at the same time. Currently I'm plowing through the three volume set, *Centennial History of the Civil War*, by Bruce Catton, while also reading a new book, *A Bohemian Brigade: The Civil War Correspondents, Mostly Rough, Sometimes Ready,* by James M. Perry.

Over time I've read dozens of books, from those marvelous volumes of Kurt Vonnegut to more serious, more "weighty" works such as Tolstoy's *War and Peace,* or Melville's *Moby Dick.* But one book in particular I've been unable to finish, *Ulysses,* by James Joyce.

I've owned a copy of *Ulysses* since I was an undergraduate back in the 60's at Rockford College where I earned my B.A. Several times I have started to read it and each time I set it aside. In frustration I purchased an abbreviated version on tape, so at least I know the general plot of the book. Perhaps some day I'll actually read the book?

My liberal arts education exposed me to a wide variety of books in many disciplines, including history, political science, economics, the classics of Greek and Rome, theatre, and anthropology. Since college, or perhaps because of college, I've been interested in the written word.

Twenty-five years ago, I resolved to read a substantial number of the works of two great 20th century American authors, John Steinbeck and Ernest Hemingway, who I had only lightly touched on in earlier years.

I obtained a library card and stalked the stacks of the small but adequate public library of Sterling, Illinois, where we lived at the time. On quiet Sunday afternoons and in the evenings after returning home from work, I read numerous books by Steinbeck and Hemingway, including *The Grapes of Wrath, East of Eden, and For Whom the Bell Tolls.* While produced decades ago, they are still relevant and filled with meaning for the 21st century.

I hope to continue reading and learning for my sake, but I also want to encourage the newest generation, that of our grandchildren, to learn to appreciate a wide range of literature, as well as history and the arts.

Part of our role as grandparents is to convey the wisdom of the ages to our grandchildren, to encourage an appreciation of the past, as well as preparing for the future.

My hope is that Sean, Michaela, Delaney, Jace, and Lucas will remember me as one who helped introduce them to some of the great values and ideas of the world, including a loving family, saving the wonders of the natural world, American history and culture, and yes, good books.

We should all get acquainted with good literature and encourage our kids and their kids to relax with a good book instead of always turning on the tube.

Do you have something to tell your family about the joys of reading?

_____

_____

_____

_____

_____

_____

_____

_____

_____

_____

_____

_____

_____

_____

_____

_____

Now a real favorite topic; money and credit.

Essay Fourteen: On Money and Credit

Keep your accounts on your thumb-nail.
*Henry David Thoreau, **Walden**, 1854*

Put not your trust in money, but put your money in trust.
Oliver Wendell Holmes,
***The Autocrat of the Breakfast Table**, 1858*

It's now clear to me that the more money you earn, the more you will spend. How many times have we heard these words? And sadly, the opposite is not always true, and thus we can easily find ourselves overextended and in financial trouble. How much money is enough and how do you learn the art of money management?

I believe there are basically two personality types that develop around money. You are destined to become either a "spender" or a "saver." And both lifestyles can work if you develop some discipline in your spending and saving habits.

My spouse, Sherry, has always been a saver. She works in the home health care field, mostly for people who we lovingly call "seniors", folks in their 70s 80s, and 90s. These people are long retired and living on Social Security, other pensions, and savings and investments. Now near the end of their lives, they are also in declining health, and need helping hands for some of life's basic chores.

Over time, I've come to meet some of her clients, who we might see in the community. Sherry has grown very fond of most of her clients, and they of her. One of the most interesting couples that I have had the opportunity to meet lived in Peotone, Illinois.

They were both quite elderly, and the wife, who suffered from Alzheimer's disease, was in her late eighties. Her husband was even older, well over ninety, and this couple must have been among the most frugal people who ever lived.

Invited to their antique filled home one evening, I recall discovering an old saying pasted on the inside door on one of their kitchen cabinets. Yellow with age it embodied their life's creed with regard to money and read:

> *Use it up*
> *Wear it out*
> *Make it do*
> *Or do without!*

These were folks who made an art out of living as inexpensively as possible. And I suppose that in retirement, living on a fixed income for decades, they really had few other options. However, I doubt that retirement was much of an adjustment because from all outward appearances, these people had always lived frugally. Most of the furnishings in their 19th century home were literally antiques, right down to the appliances.

There newest possession was their car, a ten year old Buick, which they had recently acquired when their twenty-five year old vehicle finally quit. In the basement of their home was a working cistern system that collected and stored rainwater. I fully expected there to be a functional privy in the back yard, but fortunately indoor plumbing had been added.

Linda and Clarence were the quintessential savers; turn-of – the-century folks who had lived through World War I, the Great Depression, and World War II. Their spending and saving habits were well established and unchanged by the prosperity of the 1950s. Many Boomers, raised during the economic boom, learned to become better at spending than saving.

As for credit, people raised in the first half of the twentieth century tend to distrust it. My friend, Joe, is like that. Now in his seventies, he owns one credit card, and he has only one because he used to travel frequently and did not want to carry too much cash. Hotels and car rental agencies, as we know, would rather be paid by credit card.

My own parents, now deceased, were both savers and spenders. They were financially independent in their retirement, having had the good fortune of investing in the stock market during the 1980s, a time of record growth.

As for me, I'm a reformed spender. I've learned that having too much debt is a bad thing, and with Sherry's help we've eliminated all credit cards, except for one, which is really a debit card. We've also paid off our cars, and don't plan on buying another until we can afford to self-finance such a purchase. We now have a modest but sound portfolio of investments that are not tied to the ups and downs of the stock market.

With the help of Tony, our professional financial advisor, we have established or own "bank", which is in essence a money market fund with a check writing feature. We keep a sizeable amount of funds on deposit in this "bank". These funds earn interest on deposit, and we have the ability to self-finance sizeable purchases as well. When we "borrow" from our bank, we make arrangements to pay ourselves back, with interest, thus restoring the balance.

There are other models for creating your own "bank". One is beautifully articulated by Jeffrey Reeves in his recent book: *Money for Life!...in good times and bad.* Reeves' model for a personal bank is based upon cash value life insurance. It's a fascinating concept. His entire book is focused on how we can actually free ourselves from debt. And once free from debt, we can take full charge of our money. I highly recommend his book.

I suspect that many Boomers have struggled with credit and debt. In reality, many of us have lived in two income families that were just a few paychecks away from poverty. Fortunately by now many have learned to become better at financial management, and have even become savers.

Most of us have amassed something far more valuable than money… we've developed the skills and talents that allow us to earn a reasonably good living. Apply a little discipline and we can survive financially into retirement, and pass our hard learned lessons on to future generations, as well as some material wealth.

Assuming that you wish to convey your property and wealth to your heirs, everyone should have a simple will, and update it periodically to be sure it conveys your true wishes. For some, another useful financial instrument is a living trust, which secures the dispensation of your valuables free from the time consuming probate process.

It is wise to plan for the future, one that will not burden your family with a total lack of instructions about how you wish your financial affairs to be settled.

Do you have any wisdom to impart on the topic of money management?

_____

_____

_____

_____

_____

_____

_____

_____

_____

_____

_____

_____

_____

_____

_____

_____

_____

_____

_____

_____

_____

_____

_____

_____

_____

_____

_____

_____

_____

_____

_____

_____

_____

_____

_____

Do you have a fitness plan? We all need one. Read on...

Essay Fifteen: Keeping Fit?

'Tis very certain the desire of life prolongs it.
George Gordon Lord Byron, **Don Juan**, *1819*

All would live long, but none would be old.
Benjamin Franklin, **Poor Richard's Almanac**, *1749*

Health is not a condition of matter, but of Mind...
Mary Baker Eddy, **Science and Health**, *1908*

We should pray for a sound mind in a sound body.
Juvenal, **Satires: 10:356,** *circa 115 A.D.*

Earning a living and having a meaningful relationship with a member of the fair sex seems easy compared to the topic of this little essay.

Many of us are mentally and intellectually "fit", but keeping the flesh in good tone is becoming increasingly difficult as the years take their toll and erode away our youthful vigor.

If you believe the TV info-mercials anyone can develop and keep a "hard body" well into middle age and even into old age. Just look to Jack LaLane for living proof! I suspect that few of us are willing to engage in a serious long term workout regime on one of those home gyms, or to juice yourself to youth. Some of us are just designed to be thin, trim, and fit in both appearance and reality, no matter what we eat, drink, or do.

Most of us, however, battle with our weight and never achieve real fitness, especially as we age. This is exacerbated by the fact that mostly we are engaged in sedentary "mind" work to earn our livings.

My approach to physical fitness has included working out of doors, as weather permits, on our 6 acre ranch, which affords numerous opportunities to perform maintenance chores that require some degree of physical exertion. In the past, I also used an exercise machine, a Nordic Track.

These days we take long vigorous walks several times a week, and in the warmer months I also bike regularly. I recently purchased a recumbent bicycle with 27 speeds that allows me to travel several miles into the country and back in relative comfort, while getting a good workout as well.

Sherry also has us on a reduced fat, low sodium diet, if not I'm afraid that peanuts and cheese would be my undoing. I LOVE cheese, especially the bad ones like Cheddar, Colby, and Swiss. But in moderation, even some cheese is allowable, I think.

Boomers everywhere are conscious that their weight and behavior habits can affect their health. Most of us try to control our weight, or we should, and are aware of the benefits of regular exercise and most either don't smoke, or have quit, and strive for moderation with the use of alcohol, if we use it at all.

Being a public health professional, I'm well aware of the importance of good health habits. We can all learn to take better care of the one body we have..... as we know, replacement parts come dearly, or not at all.

My friend Bill, also a public health professional, is about my age. For years he has been devoted to playing ice hockey for fun and fitness. Nearly every week he takes to the ice. I admire his steadfastness in finding and staying with a fitness plan that he also enjoys.

As you embark on a plan of regular physical fitness, remember, too, to care for and nourish your spirit as well.

Mental health and emotional well being are vital components to good overall health. I plan to continue to enjoy the remainder of my life, and to continue to pass on the wisdom which I've acquired through a long and productive life.

While I've enjoyed remarkably good health, I have been ravaged twice in recent years by bouts of serious depression. I've been well now for over 18 months, but still take medication. I want to stay well for myself, for my wife, and for my loving family.

I have been able to beat depression, but only with the help of family and friends, my primary care physician, a bevy of mental health professionals, effective medication, and lots of time, patience, and effective therapy. I'm one of the fortunate; my insurance has covered most of the cost. I'm well today and plan to stay well.

The new generation of grandchildren that we are helping to raise will surely need our support and guidance as they mature to face the daunting challenges of the 21st century on planet Earth.

We Boomers have an obligation to help assure their future success in facing questions of war, famine, and global warming in the years to come. Like you, I hope to be around a while longer.

Stay well and get fit.

So Boomers, are you staying fit?

_____
_____
_____
_____
_____
_____

_____

_____

_____

_____

_____

_____

_____

_____

_____

_____

_____

_____

_____

_____

_____

_____

_____

_____

_____

_____

_____

_____

_____

_____

_____

_____

_____

_____

Now that we've addressed fitness, let's consider our ancestors.

Essay Sixteen: Connecting with Your Roots

"Keep ancient lands, your storied pomp!"
Cries she with silent lips.
"Give us your tired, your poor,
your huddled masses yearning to breathe free,
The wretched refuse of your teaming shore.
Send these, the homeless, tempest-tossed to me,
I lift my lamp beside the golden door!
Emma Lazarus, ***"The New Colossus"****, 1883*

America is God's Crucible, the great Melting Pot
where all races of Europe are melting and reforming!
Isael Zangwill, ***The Melting-Pot****, 1908*

My folks didn't come over on the Mayflower,
but they were there to meet the boat.
Will Rogers – part native-American- circa the 1920s

We are now in the first decade of the third millennium, the
21st Century. As a modern, educated, and sophisticated
people we understand something of the past and look toward
the future with a lineal view of history. While more
primitive cultures viewed life as a series of repeating cycles,
we have been conditioned to view life as a continuum, with a
past, present, and a future. That future is constantly
unfolding, some believe as to God's plan. And while end
times have been foretold, and have come and gone, time
marches on into an uncertain future.

It is said that any understanding of the present and future
requires some understanding of what went before. And what
of the past? We each have a unique past, made up of
generations of people who preceded us, and we carry their
genes in a form of immortality that has created us from the

essence of our ancestors. I have been said to have my Grandfather Martial Empereur's ears, and certainly inherited my short build from Grandmother Genie Davis, who was barely 5 feet in height.

As a youth oriented society we have tended to dismiss our past to focus on concerns of the moment, and of the future. Yet the past, our pasts, are relevant, and should be valued as we search for meaning in our lives and our world. How did I come to be born in the middle of the 20th century in Wisconsin? How did you come to be here in this time and this place?

As Boomers who have lived for at least four decades, and longer for many, we have an emerging sense of history. Many of us have done more than wonder about the people who preceded us, those whose genes we carry forward through time.

Over twenty-five years ago, I endeavored to uncover information about the family of my paternal grandfather, Martial Joseph Empereur, (1881-1967) who I recall as a kindly, gentle, old man in my childhood, and who has been deceased now for 42 years.

The task proved difficult, for like most of us when you backtrack in time more than two or three generations, you discover that your grandparents or great-grandparents were born overseas, and spoke another language. And like many Boomers, I have ancestry from several nationalities, including English, French, and Icelandic.

With the help of Ancestry.com and some recently discovered French "cousins" I've been able to trace my French heritage back to Phillippe Empereur Poupeloz, born about 1690 and one Gabriel Empereur-Perry of another family, born about 1719. It is with the latter Empereur that I share ancestry with a contemporary French woman, Chantal Empereur.

Phillippe had children from whom my paternal great-grandfather, Pierre Maurice Empereur (1844-1895) descended.

It seems that old Gabriel had two wives, the first of which, Mauritia died leaving children from whom my paternal great-grandmother Marie Henrietta Chenal Jacquet (1847-1893) descended. His second wife, Foy Empereur Besson also bore him children from whom my French cousin Chantal Empereur descended.

I arrived on the scene in 1947, 100 years and four generations from the year of great-grandmother Marie's birth. Thus with comparative ease, I've traced my French roots back over 319 years to 17th century France.

My paternal grandfather, Martial, met and married Miss Genie Pearl Davis (1890 – 1971) in Wisconsin in about 1910. My aunt Irma Busker was a Mormon and was into genealogy long before I became a devotee. She, being a Davis before marriage, researched that lineage, tracing our roots on grandmother Genie's side back to England in 1579 to one William Seely.

Grandfather Empereur was born in the French Alps, in Sainte Foy Tarentaise, in October 1881, the son of a "cultivateur", or farmer. He immigrated to northeast Wisconsin with his parents, grandparents, and six brothers and sisters in 1891 at age 9 or 10. The family homesteaded on 80 acres between Split Rock and Marion in Shawano County, about ninety minutes drive to the north and west from Green Bay. The mile long road to the old farm bears the name Empereur Road.

I've visited the old farm three times since 1980, and it recently passed from the Empereur family. A cousin, Al Empereur purchased and still owns a portion of the land, but the old 1915 house and buildings are no longer in the family.

In today's world, no American Empereur still farms. All of the contemporary Empereur descendants elected careers in business, industry, government, and the church. The last Empereur to farm was my dad's brother, uncle George, who sold the farm near Medford, Wisconsin and moved south to Madison in the early 60's. Like my dad and all of his generation, they have now all passed away.

In many ways, my family is a metaphor for yours, and for millions of other white American families. We came to America to escape hardship, poverty, or persecution from the old world to the new. Here, we too found hardship, but we also found acceptance and opportunity for a better life on the farms and in the factories of a booming, industrializing, modernizing nation.

We became Americans, lost our foreign ways, and melted into our new adopted culture. A while back I had the opportunity to visit a refurbished Ellis Island in the New York harbor, and was struck by the majesty of the place where so many people were received to begin their new lives as Americans.

Boomers would do well to pass their family heritage on to their children. Connect with your past, and share what you find with your family. In my case, grandfather Empereur taught me something of lasting value, something that I too impressed upon our children, to reach for a better life through education.

Grampa Marshall, Sept. 1960, age 79

I've never forgotten him or his admonitions to me as a small boy to get all the "schooling" I could. In his youth, scratching out a living on a frontier farm came before schooling, and grandfather never received an education.

Subsequently, he worked at hard manual labor most of his life, on the farm, as a logger, on the railroad, and finally in a foundry. He retired just after World War II on a pension too small to afford much beyond a small house and the necessities of life.

Nevertheless, grandfather Marshall was proud and taught me well. He believed in making one's way without asking for help. As far as I know he always had work and supported a large family, and he and grandmother Genie took immense pride in their family.

Have you looked into your family history? It's an effort well worth the time.

What do you know of your family history?

_____

_____

_____

_____

_____

_____

_____

_____

_____

_____

_____

_____

_____

_____

_____

_____

_____

_____

_____

_____

_____

_____

_____

_____

_____

_____

_____

_____

_____

_____

_____

How would you tell your family story?

_____

_____

_____

_____

_____

Raymond W Empereur

Are you a risk taker? I am and I'll bet you are too...

Essay Seventeen: Risk Taking

Hitch your wagon to a star.
*Ralph Waldo Emerson, **Society and Solitude: Civilization**,*
1870

Nothing is so commonplace as to wish to be remarkable.
Oliver Wendell Holmes,
***The Aristocrat of the Breakfast Table**, 1858*

Not failure, but low aim, is crime.
*James Russell Lowell, **Under the Willow and Other Poems**,*
For the Autograph, 1968

Ambition should be made of sterner stuff.
*William Shakespeare, **Julius Caesar**, 1599*

If you think you're a second class citizen, you are.
Ted Turner, 1977

Our generation, the Baby Boomers, all 77 million born between 1946 and 1964, have been among the foremost risk-takers of modern times. You may not perceive yourself as such. However, I'm not suggesting risk taking as in engaging in activities that involve physical danger.

I'm addressing risk taking in terms of innovation and change. Change has been an operative concept and major theme in our culture since 1945. Boomers matured in an environment of rapid fire changes – social, economic, cultural, political, environmental, and technological.

A willingness to innovate in the face of uncertainty is a hallmark of success in the current business and social climate. Boomers came of age well equipped to advantage this environment. We were raised to take risks.

We are all risk takers, at least in moderation, and we take risks every day. Living implies risks – to our physical and emotional well being. For some, chance events take a toll. For others, carelessness and inattention prove to be mistakes. For yet others the risks are more subtle, such as through poor diet and poor health habits. Such health risk behaviors may in the long term result in long term harm or the onset of chronic or life threatening diseases.

And, of course, just the act of daily living may place us at risk for being a victim of someone else who is careless or worse. I'm not suggesting that we should dwell on what might happen. Most of what we worry about never comes to pass, I think.

We know there are no guarantees in life. Sometimes "fate" intervenes to hand you a lump of coal instead of a blue ribbon. And, in large measure, our fate is determined by the hand dealt us through our genetic heritage. Some will be smarter, stronger, taller, better looking or less prone to develop chronic illness or disability. Many, like me, will be pretty average.

But we can rise to most any occasion and overcome enormous obstacles and crushing adversity. Everyday we encounter people who should have failed, but didn't. These folks take risks and come out winners. And sometimes they must try over and over until they get it right.

I'm reminded of a young woman we once knew who resolved to live fully in the face of one of the worse fates that can befall a young, vigorous person. She suffered a severe spinal cord injury resulting from a car wreck that someone else caused. Confined to a wheelchair, and with little upper body movement and no ability to move her legs, she carried on. She learned to cope with daily life, bravely, and with a "can do" spirit.

She was not bitter nor did she wallow in self pity in spite of the fact that she did not deserve to be so grievously injured, and never expected to have to live under such oppressive physical limitations. How many of us could face life thus injured?

So, take some calculated risks. We learn and grow from failure and can turn adversity into success. Chances are you will come out OK and a little wiser as well.

Take it from someone who has taken major professional risks. I think I've done pretty well. But most importantly, resolve not to harm others in the process of winning your prize.

To live is to risk.

The ball's in your court again. What have you to share about taking risks?

_____

_____

_____

_____

_____

_____

_____

_____

_____

_____

_____

_____

_____

_____

_____

_____

_____

_____

_____

_____
_____
_____
_____
_____
_____
_____
_____
_____
_____
_____
_____
_____
_____
_____
_____
_____
_____
_____
_____
_____
_____
_____
_____
_____
_____
_____
_____
_____
_____

Boomers love family traditions and rituals.

Essay Eighteen: Family Rituals

Train up a child in the way he should go: and when he is old, he will not depart from it.
Proverbs, XXII, 6.

As I write this, spring is about to begin outside my window. It's mid-March, and in the chill of the morning air, the robins have returned from their winter hiatus to pluck worms from the thawing ground. Soon buds will swell on the trees and bushes and the grass will turn from brown to a beautiful green.

Easter will come in April, and I'm reminded of an earlier time when the kids were small. Not long ago, it seems, Sherry and I would rise early to hide secret Easter bunny items for the kids to find upon awakening, Or, we would hide them the night before, knowing that Chad and Marci might be up very early themselves in anticipation of the Easter Bunny's visit. And upon discovery, they would burst into the spontaneous noise of happy discovery made by kids everywhere and in every generation.

Families have an important role to play in keeping and creating rituals. As a boy, I recall our annual Easter journey to grandpa Marshall and grandma Genie's in nearby Afton, Wisconsin, on Easter Sunday. There would be a big family dinner with my cousins and aunt and uncle present, and always after dinner on a glorious spring afternoon an Easter egg hunt for us kids.

That tradition of dinner and an Easter egg hunt was carried forward by my parents, and we too have done the same for our grandchildren. As the current family elders, Sherry and I have the responsibility to be the keepers of traditions in our family.

When both sets of parents were living, Sherry and I had two sets of family rituals to keep. Max and Hazel, Sherry's parents, always loved big family gatherings at their home, which always included lots to eat. Often, so as not to disappoint either side of the family, we would try to make it to both sets of parents on a given holiday, for two celebrations and two meals. Yes, family gatherings can be taxing.

Today, due to the dispersion of families, some family rituals are more difficult to maintain. But thanks to the World Wide Web, communication with distant family members who may be anywhere in the world is relatively cheap and easy. I suspect that in the isolation caused by distance and time, many ritual family gatherings have vanished or are at best infrequent.

Over the past three years our family has developed the Empereur Family Newsletter, which I edit and produce about four times per year. And from this effort the family has begun a ritual lost since the passing of my parent's generation – annual family reunions.

Our newsletters are usually four pages of family related information and photos, and we've developed a directory with all known family names, addresses, phone numbers, and of course e-mail addresses. We use e-mail to send about half and send the remainder by regular mail, about 80 in all. In the recent past, we've also discovered living French relatives, and they are also included.

This summer a group of nine American Empereurs and their descendants will travel to France to visit our French cousins – the first face-to-face contact of American and French Empereurs since 1891 when great grandfather brought his family to the United States!

Family gatherings act as a form of "glue" to keep us connected with who we are, and include such events as celebration of major religious and secular holidays, birthdays and anniversaries, graduations, confirmations, baptisms, and family reunions. In our immediate family we have several such rituals, and also most of the immediate family is still located within 100 miles, thus making such events possible.

Every December my sister and her husband host a gathering of family and friends to remember and celebrate the life of their first born daughter, Erin, who died in 1980 as a result of accidental drowning at age three. It is in Erin's memory, and now also in the memory of her grandparents, who have also passed away, that we gather for food, fellowship, and to decorate a special living evergreen that was planted in Erin's memory in 1981. The conifer, once just a sapling has thrived over the decades and is now enormous, much too tall to place a star on the top.

Whatever the weather, we gather on a Sunday in early December to trim that enormous tree for Erin. We bundle up and venture out, arms laden with a variety of Christmas ornaments and decorations, some new and some survivors of previous winters. While my mother lived, we would also celebrate her birthday, which was in early December.

Most years we measure the tree, and hold a contest to see whose guess is closest. Once decorated, we retreat to the house and enjoy the beauty of the living tree and its symbolism. Like each of us, Erin's tree has changed over time, but each year the ritual continues.

Thus do we remember Erin and others of our family who are no longer among us.

What are your family rituals?

_____

_____

_____

_____

_____

_____

_____

_____

_____

_____

_____

_____

_____

_____

_____

_____

_____

_____

_____

_____

_____

_____

_____

_____

_____

_____

_____

_____

Have you been to the Lone Star State?

Essay Nineteen: Live from Texas - 1995

I hear America singing, the varied carols I hear…
*Walt Whitman, **I Hear America Singing.*** 1855*

"For the past hour we have been listening to the music taken largely from Grand Opera, but from now on we will present the Grand Ole Opry!"
George D. Hay, from the WSM radio show "Barn Dance" Nashville, Tennessee, December, 1927

Tuesday night. It's a warm Texas spring evening, and my daughter Marci and I have traveled a thousand miles from northern Illinois to Austin, the Capital of the Lone Star State. Tomorrow I'm participating in a work-related conference downtown and Marci has come along to keep me company. So tonight we've chosen to seek some entertainment, Austin style.

Danny, the Yellow Cab driver, thinks that this modest looking country bar on Lamar Street in south Austin may be one of the few places in the metro area with live music on a Tuesday. In our behalf, he calls a few other places on his cell phone to validate his belief. Sure enough, most road houses will have DJs tonight, not live music. So, this looks like our best bet. I decide to reconnoiter the place while Marci stands by in the cab.

Stepping inside a nearly deserted road house, I approach a waitress dressed appropriately in Texas western attire. "Yes", she answers, there will be live music tonight, and "Welcome to the Broken Spoke".

I look around the seemingly small interior, crowded with tables and chairs, nearly vacant, wondering where the band might be playing. Taking her at her word, I retreat to the cab

103

and suggest we give it a try. Marci agrees, so we thank Danny with a generous tip, asking that he return in a couple hours to return us to the downtown hotel.

Upon entering, we are greeted by a substantial server dressed in bib overalls. Asking where the music will best be heard, she escorts us to a closed door in the back, near the bar. Inside this back room is a respectively sized dance floor. On an elevated platform at the far end of the bar this evening's band is setting up and performing a sound check.

The girl singer, dressed in a full skirt and boots, smiles, checking us out: "Hum, some middle aged dude with a chick half his age", my imagination ventures. The concrete floor is ringed by small dimly lit tables. The tables are nearly all empty.

Announcing our status as tourists, we locate the souvenir T-shirt case near the back of the dancehall. Our escort seems delighted by our eagerness. Upon making our purchases, we explore the rest of this genuine Texas honky-tonk.

Across from the bar is a small room filled with glass display cases. The walls are decorated with dozens of items. This mini-museum is choked full of country music memorabilia, including instruments, photos, record albums, news clippings, and many other items. It becomes readily apparent that this modest Texas roadhouse watering hole in south Austin has a special place in the history of country music.

Here, Austin native Willie Nelson has appeared both before and since becoming a star. Here also, an amazing variety of other contemporary country music greats have performed. Among them, Dolly Parton, Marty Stuart, Travis Tritt, Randy Travis, and George Strait have all graced the stage.

We also happen upon a photo of Clint Eastwood during a visit to The Spoke. An autographed copy of James Mitchner's novel *Texas*, occupies another case.

A bit later, we enjoy a Texas tradition, ninety minutes of quality live country music, and as the evening deepens the place begins to fill with people in jeans, skirts, and business suits, boots, sneakers, and loafers intermingle. Many, if not most, appear to be from my generation. Another fact of Boomer life is that we love places like the Broken Spoke.

Upon leaving, I catch a glimpse of someone I recognize from many of the photos on display. It's none other than James M. White himself, the creator and owner for the past 31 years of this symbol of country music, Texas style.

I know why country music has appeal. Like the Broken Spoke, it's authentic Americana, unpretentious, simple, genuine, and reflecting the hopes, fears, and dreams, of the common people. Outside while waiting for our cab, one can't help to notice the melting pot of parked vehicles; pick-ups, Grand Ams, and Mercedes. Everybody loves the Broken Spoke.

The next afternoon as we deplane at O'Hare Airport, one of our fellow travelers notices Marci's new pink and black T-shirt and says with a smile, "Keep on dancing at the Spoke!"

This is the kind of story I enjoy telling. Do you have a special story about an adventure with one of your kids?

_____

_____

_____

_____

_____

_____

_____

I have a secret...do you?

Essay Twenty: Secret Lives

The automobile..... created suburbia in America.
President Lyndon B. Johnson, October 15, 1966

Every workday, Monday through Friday, for years on end we drive in our automobiles, or our vans, or our SUVs, in cars and trucks of all descriptions. We drive to and from our distant places of employment. Where such public transit exists, we commute to a train station to ride the rails with thousands of fellow travelers. We are the commuters.

We freely and gladly make these daily trips, to distant places of employment, because we choose not to live near the places where we earn our livings. Never have so many traveled so far, so rapidly or so often.

Often we seek a homestead far from the urban jungle, in the dozens of small communities, suburban neighborhoods which ring our great urban centers like Chicago, carved from land which recently produced corn, or beef, or poultry, or pork. We pursue the Great American dream of a single family home in the "burbs". Or still better, we commute to live on a mini-estate of our own, with some acreage, far from the noise, bad air, urban sprawl, and crime.

Suburbia was not invented by Boomers. Instead many of us were raised in suburban track housing that sprang up across America following the return of the GIs in 1945. As our generation came of age, the suburbanization of our country continued unabated, pulling Boomer families further from urban centers. Part of the price we pay for homes in quiet neighborhoods far from the city center is the toll we pay each day measured in the hours of our lives we spend in transit.

For many of us, these hours spent on the daily commute become personal time during which we work out our hopes, fears, and dreams. We make the best of long commutes through engaging our imaginations. Transit time becomes a time and place to work out our secret lives. We can imagine our retirement to far away places as the fence post fly by at 60 miles per hour. Or, we consider where we might spend our next vacation. Or we form our views on issues of the day, stimulated by radio programming.

I've considered virtually every subject matter imaginable on these daily trips to and from work. I've even kept a cassette recorder handy, and when so moved, record my thoughts so as not to forget them later. Some drive time is even spent planning the work day, or reflecting on the events of the day just passed. Of course, you can do business while driving via a cell phone or Blackberry, but I don't recommend it – too distracting.

And, most every day, I would spend some time listening to public radio, to a favorite CD, or FM music. On occasion, I might pass the time learning to speak French, via special language CDs, in preparation for a pending trip to France. Recently, after many years of spending from 45 minutes to an hour and 15 minutes commuting to two different jobs, we moved to within seven miles of my last full-time job. And to tell the truth, I did not miss all the time, gas, and tire tread I consumed, and the sense of guilt I was developing for consuming so many scarce resources.

With a seven mile commute, less than 20 minutes to work, what a relief I felt. Now it's even better, for I've "retired" from full time work, to work for myself as a health and human services consultant. Now I "work" at home mostly from an office I created in our den.

Well so much for commuting and the secret lives" we live out during the drive time. My wish for all Boomers is this –

find a job to your liking nearer to your home! Let's treat ourselves and the planet to less pollution and fewer greenhouse gases.

I'll bet that you are or have been a commuter. What wisdom can you share with your heirs?

_____

_____

_____

_____

_____

_____

_____

_____

_____

_____

_____

_____

_____

_____

_____

_____

_____

_____

_____

_____

_____

_____

_____

_____

_____

Be engaged in the world.... Be an activist.

Essay Twenty-One: Activism

They shall beat their swords into plowshares, and their
spears into pruning-hooks;
Nation shall not lift up sword against nation, neither shall
they learn war any more.
Isaiah, 2:4

Not everything that is faced can be changed, but nothing can
be changed until it is faced.
James Baldwin, writer and civil rights leader.

To the Baby Boom generation to have made such a deep and
permanent mark upon American social and cultural life is
due to more than the sheer size of our generation. Many
Boomers have become activists for change.

Millions, including me, have become active in political
movements, such as Move On.Org, and in a myriad of
worthy social, moral, and environmental causes. Our kids
and Generation X would do well to emulate such behavior,
for good citizenship dictates that one should contribute to
community life if we are to influence and improve the future
direction of a progressive humane society.

My activism has recently been focused on improving the
quality and availability of mental health services in my
community. I've chosen to work within the framework of
the League of Women Voters, which by the way is open to
men as well as women. Using my skills as a public health
advocate, I've helped to author a White Paper on the state of
mental health care available in my community. Our group
hopes in the long run to find ways to bring better local
funding to the current system of care, and thus improve
access to mental health services.

Of course, we all have a bit of narrow self interest at stake as well. Boomers, who comprise the bulk of the great American middle class, are worried about how the future will treat us. Will we be able to sustain our legendary high standard of living in times of economic crisis?

How will we finance our retirement? Can we count on Social Security and Medicare? What does the future hold for our children and their children? Most importantly, what sort of society and world will we leave for our heirs?

Many of us have also developed a broader view of our responsibility to the world. What has our consumer based industrial and post-industrial affluent society done to the environment? Can the damage be reversed? Hopefully science can provide some answers. One answer, the total electric car may be in the near future. So far, and with luck, we've managed to keep the planet from thermo-nuclear war.

What of the impact of population upon the planet? Was Paul Erlich right.....is the population bomb still ticking? How can western civilization continue to consume such a high percentage of earth's resources in the face of world-wide poverty?

With no lack of worthy causes, Boomers and our heirs should align ourselves with the numerous groups which advocate for specific social, political, and environmental causes. Boomers are also among the most avid environmentalists too; eager to recycle, reduced and reuse, to reduce pollution and lesson our carbon footprint where possible.

Change is imminent. We cannot continue our binge of consumption without shouldering an increasing level of responsibility to share fairly the world's resources with the millions of fellow humans who live every day in abject poverty.

We must act to achieve a balance in the world. Population growth must be curbed. Totalitarianism must be ended. War must cease.

Our generation is now briefly in control of the world. Let's resolve to leave it a better place. Take up worthy causes and encourage your children and grandchildren to do the same. Consider yourself a citizen of the world and work for justice, security, and decent health and nutrition for every nation and all people.

Things can change for the better. Teach the children. Be an example. Get engaged and involved in making a better world. Yes, we can!

Have you examples of community engagement to share with your offspring? What message do you want to convey?

_____

_____

_____

_____

_____

_____

_____

_____

_____

_____

_____

_____

_____

_____

_____

_____

_____

_____

_____

_____
_____
_____
_____
_____
_____
_____
_____
_____
_____
_____
_____
_____
_____
_____
_____
_____
_____
_____
_____
_____
_____
_____
_____
_____
_____
_____

Have you ever given money away? I have.

Essay Twenty-Two: Sixteen Dollars, or San Diego, October, 1995

When thou doest alms, let not thy left hand know what thy right hand doeth.
Matthew, VI, 3.

A while back I lost sixteen dollars in San Diego.

Actually I misspoke. It wasn't so much a loss as it was a gift. Or, maybe it was the result of being fooled, or conned, or flimflammed, hoodwinked, or deceived.

Anyway, I willingly parted with sixteen dollars that I earned from the fruits of my labor.

No, I was not robbed. I handed over the cash freely and in the spirit and act of helping someone who claimed to be in distress. Or so I thought at the moment. Yet while extending a loan of sixteen dollars it occurred to me that the odds were against ever seeing it returned to me. So why did I do it? Let me recount the brief encounter on the streets of San Diego.

This was my first, and so far my only trip to San Diego. My friend and colleague, Joe and I had arrived on a late October Saturday to attend the convention of the American Public Health Association. It was the following Monday morning and we were walking from the hotel to the Convention Center. It was a fine morning in a lovely Pacific Rim metropolis.

Suddenly at an intersection near the city center a young man approached us asking if we could help. Sincerely and skillfully he recounted a tale of misfortune. Now out of gas, he had drive into town from up the coast, having forgotten his Canadian currency back at his hotel. He claimed to be stranded due to a faulty gas gauge and needed some gas money, $16 to be exact, to purchase a gas can and some fuel to allow him to get back. So far everyone he had approached had turned him down. Joe backed away, clearly not falling for his story. But I felt a tinge of compassion.

Gazing at this fellow, he appeared credible. Twentyish, in wire frame glasses, casually dressed, but neat and clean, our supplicant did not give the appearance of a vagrant, of a homeless person, or an alcoholic. And he promised to repay, if I would be kind enough to assist. He even sounded like Canadians I had known.

What to do? Two choices presented: to turn away, or to step up to the plate.

When confronted with adversity, one is inclined to internalize the problem presented, to develop empathy. Clearly, our young friend knew we looked like out-of-towners ourselves. And, while he may have been truthful, everyone on the streets of a big city asking for money is immediately suspect.

My good Samaritan instinct won me over. I gave the fellow the sixteen dollars and my name and address, just in case his story was legitimate. He thanked me and we parted, he supposedly to buy gas for his car, and Joe and I to make the opening session of the convention.

As we walked away, Joe opined that I would never see the money returned. I joked that our needy friend was actually a multi-millionaire testing the kindness of human nature, or some graduate student engaged in behavioral research at UCLA. Sure, I said, I would get my money back.

I suspected otherwise and indeed the money was never returned. Still, I felt that I had won. I had acted out of kindness to a believable story of misfortune.

Maybe we should all give a little money to strangers in need. What can it hurt?

But, if you ever encounter a down-on-his-luck Canadian anywhere in San Diego, <u>beware.</u>

So, have you ever acted to give aid to someone, and wondered if you were being taken for a fool?

Do you have a Good Samaritan story to share?

_____

_____

_____

_____

_____

_____

_____

_____

_____

_____

_____

_____

_____

_____

_____

_____

_____

_____

_____

_____

_____

_____

_____

_____

_____

_____

_____

_____

_____

_____

Do you keep a diary, or write in a journal?

Essay Twenty-Three: Journaling

"One of the best ways to learn to enjoy writing, is to do it on a regular basis. I recommend keeping a personal journal, a diary of your life and times."

Larry Berlin, University of Michigan, 1990

It was Larry Berlin, an instructor in the Master of Public Health program at the University of Michigan, Ann Arbor, whom I credit with getting me started keeping a journal. Once I began, using Word Perfect, and now MS Word on my home computer, I never stopped. At the time, I was the executive director of the Will County Health Department in Joliet, Illinois, and had decided to return to school for a second master's degree in public health.

That was 19 years ago, and while I have at times neglected making weekly entries, I also have always returned to the format. I'm currently in Volume XVII of my journal, meaning that I have made 16 editions and am now in the 17th. Over time, I've composed several hundred pages of reflections on my life and times.

My usual mode has been to stop at a point in time, usually at the end of a calendar year, save the file to both the hard drive and now to a "flash" drive, then print out a paper copy and place it in a three ring binder for storage and for easy reference. Then I begin yet another volume on the word processor. Most editions represent a calendar year.

Why do I do this? Mostly I enjoy doing it. And when I look back, as I occasionally do, I'm struck with how many of life's events that would be totally forgotten if not written into a journal as a permanent record. Journaling also gets me into the habit of writing, and more proficient at using the written word, both for pleasure and in my work.

Organizing one's journal is very simple. I just note the date and day of each entry and then begin, like this: March 21, 2009 – Saturday, followed by my entry for that day. Knowing that what I write will be available for others to read, tempers my language, topics and the detail to which I go in composing my entries. Some times what you really feel like writing could be hurtful to others. Thus, I write for an audience, mostly the family, present and future, who might care to read all or portions of my compositions.

I also import other things into the journal, including letters, portions of my book on the Baby Boom generation, or the family newsletters that I prepare on a quarterly basis. Photos can also be copied and entered as you like.

Here's the first few pages of my current journal, as an example of how your journaling can be done:

JOURNAL- VOLUME XVII:
A RECORD OF EVENTS IN THE LIFE
OF THE EMPEREUR FAMILY
OF WINNEBAGO COUNTY, ILLINOIS

FROM JANUARY 1, 2009
THROUGH …. (To be determined)

By

Raymond W. Empereur

January 3, 2009 – Saturday

Happy New Year! We spent New Year's Eve at Burkharts. The Hunts joined us. We three couples each contributed a pizza to share. We brought some sparkling grape juice too. We stayed till about 10:00 PM, playing several games of Uno. On Tuesday, I met with Joel C. at the College of Medicine. He has asked me to draft a reply to an RFP for a community needs assessment. Since then I've spent 14 hours drafting it and have another hour to get the draft done in final form. It's due on the 9th, and I expect to have it ready for Joel to review by the 5th.

Yesterday we sat for little Lucas, while the rest of the family went to see "Marley and Me." He was plenty fussy, and cried much of the time. He had never before been left with us. In spite of his bad temper, we still enjoyed the little man, and I got to feed him too. Today we journeyed up to Juda, Wisconsin, watched two of Delaney's basketball games – they won both. Then we drove to Freeport to see Marci's beautiful new office. She worked today to help with the move.

After lunch at Culver's we drove home, looked up several houses for sale and drove by four, one of which we liked and hope to see soon.

We pulled our house off the market on Tuesday and won't re-list it until March. We've been on the market since October 2007 still no closing!

January 10, 2009 – Saturday

I'm at the PC nursing a cold beer at 2:22 PM, waiting for the kids and grandkids to arrive. I'm officially celebrating my 62nd birthday. It's a snowy day. We've had over 5 inches in the past 24 hours and the snow only recently stopped. In fact the threat of snow put a stop to plans to dine at Fiesta Cancun last evening with the Burkharts and Hunts.

Things are going very well so far in 09, except that we've been unable to close on our house and move. I have steady work, at least through August from Health Systems Research. I'm also beginning a part-time project for the Illinois Public Health Association, and expect to get more work from Frana and Co. So I'm well pleased that Empereur Consulting is a success.

I'm looking forward to seeing family this afternoon, and so far (except for arthritis in my hands) my health is quite good, including my mental health!

Well, the beer's about gone and I think I'll join the Mrs. in the living room as we await our kids.

As you see, I use a casual narrative style in composing my journal. Style and format matter little. Use what is comfortable for you. So, do you want to begin a journal? Have at it, and enjoy the experience.

I do heartily recommend keeping a journal. Why not try it for a month. Just develop the discipline to make at least one entry per week. I think you'll find it good for the soul, and good practice in writing as well.

_____

_____

_____

_____

_____

_____

_____

_____

_____

_____

_____

Essay Twenty-Four: Our Heroes

*The significant problems we have cannot be solved at the
same level of thinking with which we created them.*

Albert Einstein

Paul Simon is my hero.

I think most Boomers can identify at least one hero; at least
one person, living or dead, whom we associate with
greatness for one reason or another.

Actually I admire both men with the well known name of
Paul Simon; one is still living, the other died in December
2003. Neither is a Boomer.

One was a liberal Illinois politician, the other is a world class
musician and composer, best known for his collaboration
with Art Garfunkel in the duo Simon and Garfunkel.

Paul Simon, the musician, was born in 1941, and at nearly 68
is still actively recoding and performing. Paul Simon, the
popular U.S. Senator was born in 1928 and died at age 75 in
Springfield following complications from heart surgery.

Senator Paul Simon was a native of Oregon, and at the age of
19 became the nation's youngest editor-publisher when he
took control of the Troy Tribune, Troy, Illinois in 1947, the
year of my birth. Simon eventually built a chain of 13
newspapers in central and southern Illinois. He sold his
interest in the newspapers in 1966, the year Sherry and I
were married, to devote full-time to public service and
writing.

By then, Simon was already an established politician, having been elected to the Illinois House and 1954, when I was 7, and to the Illinois Senate in 1962, when I was 15.

Elected lieutenant governor of Illinois in 1968, when I was a college senior, he was the first Democrat to be elected with a Republican governor. He narrowly lost his bid for the gubernatorial primary to Dan Walker in 1972. That year we moved from Peoria back to Rockford, our home town.

Simon started the public affairs reporting program at Sangamon State University in Springfield. He lectured during the 1972 -73 school year at the Kennedy School of Government at Harvard. In 1972, our daughter Marci was born. Son Chad was 3 years old.

Paul Simon was elected to the U.S. House of Representatives in 1974, serving Illinois' 22nd and 24th Congressional Districts for ten years. In 1984, he upset three-term incumbent conservative Republican Charles Percy to win election to the U.S. Senate. In 1987-88, he sought the Democratic nomination for president. In 1987, I took the job of executive director of the Will County Health Department in Joliet.

Simon won re-election to the Senate in 1990, defeating Congresswoman Lynn Martin of Rockford with 65% of the vote. During his Congressional career, Simon became known for exceptional constituent service, and for honesty and straight-talk.

He elected to retire from Congress in 1997, after two terms in the Senate, to become founder and director of the Public Policy Institute at SIU's Carbondale, Illinois campus. At the end of 1997, I took early retirement from Lake County Health Department in Waukegan, Illinois, to pursue a doctorate and begin a consulting career.

Now known as the Paul Simon Public Policy Institute, the organization he founded differentiates itself from similar organizations by working directly with elected officials to create and implement changes in public policy.

Knowing my affinity for the field of public administration, it is not too difficult to understand my admiration for Paul Simon. I was privileged to meet the Senator in 1999, as the keynote speaker at the Annual meeting of the Illinois Public Health Association.

The image of Senator Paul Simon is of a neat man in horn-rim glasses and his famous bow tie and jacket. He spoke in a deep voice in a slow and deliberate manner. He was smart, articulate, and above all honest.

He believed, as do I, that government should be an advocate for the people. He believed that government has a role to play in creating a just and fair society. Paul Simon was a model of integrity, not beholden to special interests.

Oh, that we could have more like him in public service. Paul Simon, my hero.

Well, I expect we all have a hero. Who is yours, and why?

_____

_____

_____

_____

_____

_____

_____

_____

_____

_____

Summing Up

That brings to end my few pages of "wisdom" for the ages, at least for now. I hope that you, too, can find your voice and plan to produce your own memoir. Take your time to plan your written legacy to be sure to produce a work that you'll be proud to leave behind.

Together, we've taken a brief excursion through the mind and soul of one typical Boomer. We've glimpsed at what makes some Boomers tick, some of what motivates us, and some of what we value.

Boomers, I expect you'll agree, are a little like every other generation, and yet we're quite unique.

Boomers occupy a special place in our culture. There will likely never be a group as large or as homogenous in all of American history.

We embody all that is good, all that is average, and all that is bad about human nature. We are filled with contradictions; simultaneously creative and destructive. We have the power to save the planet or to destroy it.

But mostly, Boomers are hopeful, optimistic, capable, and future oriented. Let's not let our kids and grandkids down.

Like it or not, Boomers are currently leading the nation, and the world.....into the brave new world of the future.

Ray W. Empereur
Rockford, Illinois
April 2009